Murphy and Shayna,

The Story of Two Good Friends

And Much, Much More

Greta Marsh

Murphy and Shayna,
The Story of Two Good Friends

Greta Marsh

Copyright © 2016 Greta Marsh

Published by 1st World Publishing
P.O. Box 2211, Fairfield, Iowa 52556
tel: 641-209-5000 fax: 866-440-5234
email: worldlibrary@lisco.com
web: www.1stworldpublishing.com

First Edition
LCCN: 2016912885
Softcover ISBN: 978-1-4218-3762-8
Hardcover ISBN: 978-1-4218-3764-2

This material has been written and published for educational purposes to enhance one's well-being. In regard to health issues, the information is not intended as a substitute for appropriate care and advice from health professionals, nor does it equate to the assumption of medical or any other form of liability on the part of the publisher or author. The publisher and author shall have neither liability nor responsibility to any person or entity with respect to loss, damages, or injury claimed to be caused directly or indirectly by any information in this book.

Acknowledgement

It was in 1993 that I first wrote "Murphy and Shayna: The Story of Two Good Friends." Ten years later, in March and April 2003, I edited and expanded it. This required time and concentration and I thank Diana and Danny Boy, two precious Greyhounds, for their patience and understanding most of the time. I repeat: Most of the time.

There were times when Diana would complain, sometimes with soft and at other times with very loud Eeeee Eeeees. This is the same language Shayna sometimes used when she wanted my attention. Diana, however, uses it more frequently. These Eeeee Eeeees mimic the noise a squeaky toy makes when someone squeezes it. But Diana's (and Shayna's) Eeeee Eeeees definitely aren't noise. They are one of several ways of communicating.

As for tall, dark and handsome Danny Boy, he'd frequently walk into the computer room with a toy in his mouth. When I responded by playing with him for several minutes, he'd be content. When I did not, he'd drop his toy, whine softly for a while, then bark. Loud! In a deep baritone voice! He knew that doing so would get my attention. And he was right! It always did. Diana's bark, on the other hand, is high pitched and usually accompanied by a wrinkling of her gorgeous black nose.

Since I named Danny Boy after one of my favorite songs, I'll conclude by saying, Oh Danny Boy, Oh Danny Boy and Diana — I love you so.

Greta
April 2003
Easthampton, MA

Dedication

To everyone who is homeless or has been abused,
Whether you have four feet or whether you have two,
This book is dedicated with love to you.

In loving memory of Michael Parnofiello.
Your physical body was destroyed in a violent
accident but you did not die.
You are my dear beloved one and you never shall die.

Introduction

This is a story in rhyme about two good friends. It is about Murphy and Shayna who, after traveling vastly different roads, find friendship, love, respect and safety in a new home.

This story also is about homelessness and abuse, both of which cross the barrier that separates human animals from animals of other species, also known as non-human animals. Homelessness is homelessness and abuse is abuse whether their victims have four feet or two and regardless of the language they use to communicate their thoughts and feelings. It has been well documented, indeed it's an established fact that humans who abuse, torture and murder non-humans eventually do the same to humans. Please do not befriend such persons. Indeed, keep far away from them.

Some readers may ask why this story was written in verse. I don't know why. It just happened. I do hope, after reading this story, that you will feel respect and compassion, perhaps even love, for Murphy and Shayna and for all animals of all species everywhere.

Greta
April 2003

9

Part One

For Adults
and
Children Eight to Twelve Years of Age

Chapter One
Shayna's Bed

"Murphy, Murphy," Shayna said,
"Please go away. This is my bed."
Murphy ignored Shayna, so she gave him a nudge.
When he refused to move, Shayna started to whine.
It was clear she was saying, "This bed is mine."

She placed one graceful leg upon her bed
and with the other gently touched Murphy's head.

"Go away," Murphy said, "leave me alone.
Why don't you chew on your nylabone?"
"I don't want my bone. I want my bed.
I'm sleepy and tired," Shayna said.

"Murphy, Murphy, you tore up your bed.
Now please don't do the same to mine
because I really like my pretty bed.
I like it a lot. I like it just fine."

Shayna usually was gentle and kind.
That Murphy shared her bed she didn't mind.
But to use it and use it all the time was too
much, she said, "especially since it's mine."

"Murphy, Murphy, go away.
This is not your bed," I heard Shayna say.
"Murphy, Murphy, it's just not fair
that you lie on my bed and get it full of your hair."

"Oh, c'mon Murphy," I then heard Shayna say,
"It's such a nice day, a beautiful day,
a perfect day to go out and play.
So let's go."

Chapter Two

Meet Murphy

As for size, Murphy certainly was not small.
In fact, he was large and somewhat tall.
Murphy was long-haired and reddish-gold.
When he was adopted he was about two years old.

He had lived on the streets. At first no one knew why.
Had he been lost or abandoned? Both are reasons to cry.
To be homeless is sad, but it doesn't mean you're bad.
Being homeless made Murphy a very sad lad.

Becoming homeless can happen to anyone.
And one thing is certain: it sure isn't fun.
What is it Murphy? You have something to say?
Murphy wants to tell us about a terrible day
in his life.

Chapter Three

Murphy's Story

"The persons I lived with abandoned me.
They moved away. They left me alone
and for about a year I was on my own.

"Although I pretended not to care,
I really did. Of course I did.
What they did to me was so unfair.

"They moved away without saying a word.
They took everyone else, including the bird.
I didn't know why and I started to cry.
I cried and cried. It's obvious why.

"I thought they loved me, but I was wrong.
They obviously didn't and now I had to be strong.

"I had lived with them in a real nice home.
I had a family I used to call my own.
Then one day a moving van parked at our door.
Soon after that my family drove away.
I saw them no more.

"They took everyone else, but me they didn't take.
They left me behind. I thought my heart would break.
What they did to me was cruel and unkind.
They should not have moved and left me behind.

"It was a really scary and awful day,
the day they left and moved away.
I then lived on the streets for almost a year,
a year filled with sadness, hunger and fear.

"One day I was caught and brought to a shelter where
I was placed in a cage where I spent some time
living like a prisoner. Yet I had committed no crime.
Unless it's a crime to have no home,
and have no one to love and call your own.

"Some shelters aren't friendly places.
They're crowded and filled with lots of strange faces.
And it doesn't matter if you have four feet or two.
Living in a shelter isn't good for you
                        or for someone you love,
                        or for someone you know,
                        or for any someone.

"To be homeless is scary if you have four feet or two.
I sure was scared and you would be too."

Chapter Four

Murphy's Story Continued

But the shelter couldn't keep Murphy much longer,
so a caring lady placed an ad in a paper.
The ad begged and pleaded for a home
for a dog who was doomed unless he got one soon.
Very Soon!

After reading this ad Greta knew
that if she didn't adopt Murphy he surely was through.
So she called the shelter right away
and said she'd come for him that very same day.

Murphy was frightened, nervous and sad.
Yet he'd done nothing wrong, he hadn't been bad.
People were responsible for the trouble he was in.
To be homeless is scary, but it sure isn't a sin.

"What my guardians did was cruel and unkind.
They should not have moved and left me behind.
Did they really think I would not mind?
Or was it simply that they didn't care?
Whatever their reasons, they were mean and unfair.

"Living on the streets is a scary thing
whether you're a dog or a cat or a human being.
It doesn't matter if you're an adult or a child.
Living on the streets can drive you wild.

"It's scary enough if your name is Mary or John.
But if your name is Scampi, Rum Tum or Rover,
then it's pretty certain your life soon will be over.
No, it doesn't matter if you have four feet or two.
Being homeless is scary when it happens to you,
                    or to someone you love,
                    or to someone you know,
                    or to any someone.

"Too many dogs and cats have no home.
They have no one to love and call their own.
They suffer in silence. No one hears them cry.
When their time at the shelter is up they must die.
So please, young readers, without any fuss,
come with your parents to a shelter and adopt one of us.

"Shayna, sometimes you tell me to go away.
You say you're just not in the mood to have fun and play.
But when I'm being silly, I'm feeling free,
and that's such a change from how I used to be."

Chapter Five

Meet Shayna

Shayna's hair was short. She was brindle and white.
She was quite beautiful, an elegant sight.
Her body was all muscle, her legs long and thin.
She'd been a racing dog who for years did win
a lot of money for her trainer and others at the track.

That was all they wanted. It couldn't have been plainer.
You see, when Shayna started to slow down when she was almost four,
her trainer screamed and shouted, "Run faster! Win more!"

But almost four isn't young for a racing dog.
Shayna did her best, but when she finally slowed down,
her trainer's smile turned into a frown.
You see, Greyhounds must win or else many will die.
To call racing a sport is a terrible lie.

Please listen young readers! Hush girls and boys!
Be very quiet. Put away your toys.
Shayna too wants to talk to you.

Chapter Six

Shayna's Story

"I started to race at eighteen months old.
I was very fast, so I was told.
I raced on the best tracks. They were graded A.
And I suppose you could say I was treated OK.

"But when I started to slow down after turning three,
I was shipped to tracks that were graded B.
                              then C.
                              then D.

"C and D tracks are not good.
I'd have run much faster if I could.
Honest I would! I really would!
If only I could! If only I could!

"My brain said Go! But my body said No!
I tried my best, but I raced too slow.
Life at the track is no piece of cake.
Racing too often makes your body ache.

"People paid money to see us run.
They thought it was a lot of fun
especially when their numbers won.
This is all we were to everyone:
                                    Money Machines!
                                    Money Machines!
                                    Money Machines!

"At the low grade tracks the food smelled bad.
Some friends became ill, which made us mad and sad!
Also scared!
And when some of them died, the rest of us cried,
                                    and cried,
                                    and cried.

"I'll never forget the trainers' faces
when we racers slowed down and stopped winning races.
The looks on their faces were not very nice.
The looks on their faces were cold as ice.

"At such times we felt as helpless as tiny mice
when they're caught in traps that are set by persons.
Those traps aren't nice. They sure aren't nice.
                            They sure aren't nice.

"There were some trainers who appeared to care.
They wanted to help us. They were decent and fair.
They wanted to set up a retirement farm
so that retired racers would come to no harm.

"But the others laughed and called them fools.
Greyhounds, they said, were money-making tools.
Nothing more! Just money-making tools!
To them that is all we were.

"The muzzles we wore didn't feel very good.
They were made of metal and felt as hard as wood.
We wore them practically all the time.
We wore them because we had no choice.
We wore them because we had no voice.

"Yes, people paid money to see us race.
They seemed to have a lot of fun.
But they didn't hear us when we cried
and didn't know how or when we died.

"Some trainers beat racers after they lost a race.
It hurts to have bruises on your body and face.
My trainer decided, when I was almost four,
that I was too slow and would race no more.

"I heard trainers talk, heard some of them say,
'Why bother to feed them when they're no good to us?
Let's get rid of them fast, in any old way.
Let's get rid of them fast, without any fuss.'
And mine did.

"He drove me to a lonely spot, left me there and drove away.
I found myself in a cemetery, a lonely place.
My racing muzzle was still on my face
and so I couldn't eat scraps and by the time I was found
I was one very frightened and sick Greyhound.

"The industry tells us to win or die.
To call racing a sport is a terrible lie.

"But I was lucky.
An animal control officer found me and then
took care of me until I was well again.
She hugged and kissed me and it felt so good.
I'd have hugged and kissed her back if only I could.
If only I could.

"But I didn't know how. I do know now and
I love that lady. I love her very much.
I'll always remember her gentle touch.

"She brought me to a Greyhound adoption group.
The people there found me a wonderful home.
Greta adopted me and taught me about love.
Now I'm no longer frightened, hungry or alone.

"But not all racers are as lucky as I.
Many suffer injuries and cannot be saved.
They could not be saved no matter how hard we prayed.
And when I think about them, as I often do ....."
Shayna let out a great big sigh .....
"My heart starts to ache and I start to cry.

"Some suffer heart attacks while racing on the tracks,
seizures too, and broken necks and bones.
They don't live long enough to make it to new homes.

"Racers must win in order to live.
When they stop winning and have no more to give,
some are discarded in ways that aren't nice,
in ways that are scary and not very nice.
You see, this business makes people cold as ice.
                              Cold as ice.
                              Cold as ice.

"Dog racing is bad! It should not be!
What they do to us most persons don't see.
It's called a sport, but I don't know why."
Shayna paused for a moment and I heard her sigh.
"The abuse is awful. It's frightening too.
You never know when it will happen to you
                    or to someone you love.
                    or to someone you know.
                 or to any someone.

"Abuse is awful if you have four feet or two.
It's a terrible thing when it happens to you,
                    or to someone you love.
                    or to someone you know.
                 or to any someone.

"My life at the track now is in the past.
Yet it continues for others who must run very fast
if they are to continue to live.
But many cannot. They have nothing left to give.

"Sooner or later we all slow down.
That's how it is. It can't be helped.
No one can be a winner forever.

"If people learned the truth, what would they do?
Would they attend the races as they did before?
Or would they stay away and say, No More!?
I hope they'd stay away if they only knew.
Now that you know the truth, young readers,
What would you do?
Tell me young readers, what would you do?

"Murphy, life now is good living with Greta and you,
but I still think about racers who continue to die …."
Now Shayna broke down and started to cry.

"Dog racing must go! It should not be!
Not just because of what it did to me,
but also because of what it still does to others:
those gentle Greyhounds, my sisters and brothers."

Murphy tried to comfort Shayna.
She was in pain. It couldn't be plainer.

"Murphy, Murphy, I don't mean to be mean.
But I suppose sometimes that's what I may seem.
At such times I'm thinking about my past,
when my life depended upon running fast.
I know I've talked about it before,
but like you, I need to talk some more."

Chapter Seven

Murphy and Shayna at Home

Murphy is lucky. He has a thick coat of hair.
He loves to run everywhere.
Greyhounds are a different matter.
To tolerate the cold they'd have to be fatter.
They have a lot of muscle and are long and lean.
They're gentle and loving and certainly not mean.

These two good friends love to run.
They like being outdoors where they have lots of fun.
But they're not permitted to go off on their own.
Unless someone is with them they must stay at home.

Sometimes when the weather was cold and freezing
Shayna knew if she went out she'd end up sneezing.
"I know I would Murphy, and perhaps you would too.
So let's think of something that we can do
Indoors!"

They thought and thought; then Greta had an idea.
"We can go into the barn where you can run for a while,
and have fun in the horses' wood shavings pile.
I don't think Baron and Brody will mind at all,"
Greta said with a great big smile.

"Or would you rather stay here?
I'll switch on more lights so we can better see.
Then, if you like, I'll toss you a ball.
C'mon you two, decide and tell me."

"Greta, Greta, I don't care and
I don't like your underwear,"
silly Shayna said with a silly smirk.
That Greyhound sure was some piece of work.

"Shayna, this is a serious matter.
It's not the time for foolish chatter,"
Murphy said gently to his friend.
He was hoping that her foolishness would end.

"Murphy, Murphy I don't care
and I don't like **your** underwear,"
Shayna replied with that same silly smirk.
Yes, that Greyhound sure was some piece of work.

Murphy liked to keep busy and on the go,
but what he wanted to do now, he didn't know.
Then Shayna spoke and I heard her say,
"I know what I want to play today.
I want to play Shoes!"

"Shoes! Shoes! Did you say Shoes?"
Murphy and Greta asked. They were confused.
But pretty Shayna said not a word.
She disappeared and not a sound was heard.

In less than a minute Shayna was back
carrying in her mouth a shoe that was black.
She dropped off the shoe in the big bedroom,
then she trotted away and was back very soon
with a boot!

She did this over and over again
until there were a total of ten
Shoes and Boots! Boots and Shoes!
Whose Boots? Whose Shoes?
Why Greta's of course. That's whose!

Some were quite worn and very old.
Others were to protect her from the cold.

"Oh follow me, follow me. Please come and see."
Shayna's request was more like a plea.
So Greta did what Shayna bid.
She went into the bedroom and saw on the floor
some boots and shoes! Her boots and shoes!

Shayna sat near them on the floor.
She smiled and asked, "Shall I get some more?"
Murphy and Greta smiled because who could frown?
Shayna was such an adorable clown.

The three of them started to laugh and then
caught their breath and laughed again and again.

Chapter Eight
More about Shayna at Home

Often while Greta watched TV,
Shayna would say, "That's no fun for me."
Quietly she'd trot out of the room
then reappeared again very soon.
Sometimes she carried a tall rubber boot.

What a clown she was - so charming and cute!
She carried it into the big bedroom
and dropped it with a loud boom-boom!
Shayna repeated this over and over and over again.

"Shayna, Shayna, please do stop.
These are boots and shoes that I can use."

"I'm only throwing them up in the air.
I'm not hurting them Greta. C'mon be fair."

"Oh all right Shayna, but please keep it quiet.
You make so much noise it sounds like a riot."
Shayna was proud of what she had done.
What's more, she'd had a lot of fun.

She was pleased with herself and wagged her tail.
She wagged it so hard against the wall
it sounded like someone was bouncing a ball.
Her wagging tail made a lot of noise,
as if someone was playing with a lot of toys.

Chapter Nine

More about Murphy At Home

Now Murphy didn't want to be outdone.
He too liked to have some fun.
So he looked for and found a small scatter rug.
He threw it high into the air, caught it and then
he threw it up again and again.

His favorite game was throwing this rug.
Perhaps because it always got him a hug.
He'd do this a few more times and then
he'd jump into Shayna's bed again.

He'd stare at Shayna with a mischievous look.
Shayna pretended to be angry. Murphy pretended to cry.
He howled and let out a very loud sigh.
So loud that Greta came running to see
what the cause of that howling and sighing could be.

It was all in fun, they both were okay.
In fact, Murphy and Shayna had started to play.

Then Greta spoke:
"I really don't like the noise you two make.
Sometimes it feels as if the walls are starting to shake.
C'mon, Murphy, c'mon, Shayna too,
you know how much I love the two of you.

"But look at this room! It's an awful sight!
In fact, it's a mess and that is not right.
You've gone a little too far and I'm not feeling glad."
Murphy and Shayna now felt very bad.

"I'm sorry," said Shayna. Murphy said, "Me too.
We don't want to do things that are stressful to you.
But sometimes we seem to get carried away.
It's not that we're thoughtless. We just like to play.
Sometimes we're too rough. We'll cut out the rough stuff."

"We love you," said Shayna, "you know we do.
And we know that you love the two of us too."

Greta loves them a lot and is very kind.
She understands and usually doesn't mind
when Murphy and Shayna bark and play rough
because she knows it's in friendship and not serious stuff.

She knows their barks have meaning and are not noise.
Please remember this, girls and boys.
Barking has meaning. It is not noise.

Chapter Ten

The Sounds That Dogs Make

Have you ever thought about the sounds that dogs make,
I mean barking and whining and growling and such?
Well, those sounds have meaning. They are very real.
Dogs use them to express what they think and feel.

Their thoughts and feelings are just as real
as the thoughts and feelings people think and feel.
Nonsense they're not, girls and boys!
Dogs' sounds have meaning. They are not noise!

It's the same with respect to all living creatures.
They make sounds in order to communicate.
The sounds they make are their way of talking.
Please remember this, girls and boys.
The sounds they make are not noise!

Chapter Eleven

Murphy in the Morning

In the morning Murphy was the first to awake.
He awoke very early and was careful not to make
any noise that would disturb the rest of the house.
Why, Murphy could be as quiet as a mouse.

But sooner or later he'd go over to Shayna.
She'd bark at him because she wanted to sleep.
She'd bark at him without opening an eye.
She'd growl at him too. Murphy didn't know why.

This playful young man didn't have a clue.
Tell me, young readers, tell me, do you?
Let me explain: Shayna didn't like to get up early
so when Murphy woke her up she became rather surly.

He'd whisper something in her ear.
Whatever it was she didn't want to hear.
"Don't wake me Murphy! Let me be!
When I get up is up to me!"

But when Shayna and Greta finally were up and about,
Murphy was so happy he'd bark and shout,
and wag his tail and jump about.

"Hooray! Hooray! It's time to eat,"
he barked as he jumped and kicked up his feet.
Whenever Murphy jumped he jumped so high
it seemed like he just might reach the sky.

With his big brown eyes that shone so bright,
Murphy was quite a magnificent sight.
Breakfast was his favorite meal.
Perhaps because it made him feel
So Great!

At breakfast and dinner Murphy ate
until there was nothing left on his plate.
Shayna also liked to eat.
But the three of them never ate any meat.
They believed that eating other animals was wrong.
So they ate a plant based diet and were healthy and strong.

Chapter Twelve
Murphy's and Shayna's Treats

Whenever Greta was going away
for an hour or two or part of a day,
Murphy and Shayna lined up in a row
just to make sure that Greta would know.....
just to make sure that she'd not forget
to give them each a special treat.
How Neat!

Greta never forgot, she'd always remember,
whether it was January or June, or the month of
September.
Shayna would trot into the bedroom where
she munched and crunched on her delicious fare.

Murphy ate his in no special place.
Then he'd run over to Shayna and the frown on her face
told him he'd better get out of her space.

The same thing happened when Greta came home.
They got another treat for being so neat and not
messing their home when they were home alone.

Chapter Thirteen

When Day is Done

Every day when day is done
and the night that follows has already come,
when the sun is away until the next day,
when it's very late, when it's going-to-bed time,
Murphy and Shayna think that's just fine.

But before settling down, their teeth must be brushed.
It's something they like and never is rushed.
You see, dogs' teeth are like yours and mine.
Keep them clean and they'll stay healthy and fine.

Now Murphy and Shayna are quite content
living in a home filled with love and respect.
But when they think of old friends they sometimes cry.
They ask over and over, "Why did they die?"

Because they were homeless? Because they no longer won?
Those never are reasons to hurt anyone.
But most of the time these two feel okay.
In fact, the other day I heard Shayna say,
"I'm so glad that you're a friend of mine."

Yes, the other day while they went for a walk.
I listened carefully and heard them talk.
Said Shayna to Murphy, "I'm glad you're my friend.
I love you Murphy and I will to the end.
I will. It's true. I'll always love you."

Said Murphy to Shayna, "You're my best friend.
Ours is a friendship that never will end.
I love you Shayna, I really do.
Honest I do. I do love you."

The End of Part One

Now you know the story of two good friends.
But I want you to know before Part One ends,
Greta bought Murphy another bed.
His is gold. Shayna's is red.

Part Two

**For Everyone
Twelve Years of Age and Older**

Chapter 14

Shayna Remembers
More of Her Past

"Shayna, Shayna," Murphy said,
"please don't sit on my new bed.
This one's for me, you know it is.
So move away and let me be."

"Murphy, don't be such a selfish guy.
Remember how often on my bed you'd lie?
Or did you forget? I don't think you did.
So stop being such a mean, old kid."

"I love you Shayna," Murphy said.
"But please, oh please get out of my bed.
You have your own. You don't need mine too.
Surely one bed is enough for you.
When I'd lie on your bed you'd have a fit.
You didn't like it. Not one bit!"

"You're right, my friend," I heard Shayna say
while they talked together the other day.
"You probably think I'm being greedy.
If I am it's because I'm still very needy.

"I just can't forget those awful days when
I was confined to a small and dirty pen.
The food they fed us was diseased and raw.
It made our bellies painful and sore.
Some Greyhounds died from eating this food.
Their dying put the rest of us in a very sad mood.

"I try to forget those awful years
that were so very scary and filled with fears.
I try, but it's something I cannot do.
I want to. I want to. I really do.
But it's something I'm just not able to do.

"Tell me Murphy. Tell me. Can you?
Can you forget those dreadful times,
those dreadful years when no one cared,
when nobody heard you when you cried,
and would not have cared if you had died?

"I want to forget, but it's something I cannot do.
Tell me Murphy, can you? Can you?"

Chapter 15

Murphy Remembers More of His Past

"I wish I could Shayna, I wish I could.
I would if I could Shayna, I would if I could.
I too have talked about my life before,
and I too need to talk some more.

"While living on the streets I felt sad and blue.
There wasn't anyone I could turn to.
There was no one nearby to guide me or tell me
what I should do.

"Danger was close by. It was everywhere.
I learned that life wasn't always fair.
I lived on the streets. What else could I do?
I didn't like it there, but what could I do?
Tell me dear readers, what would you do?
What would you do?

"Life wasn't easy. It was hard and sad.
Remembering makes me feel more than a bit
mad.
I tried to be brave, even pretended to be glad,
but in truth I was awfully, awfully scared.
I cried a lot, asleep and awake.
I was certain that my heart would break.

"The streets are exactly what they seem:
scary and mean, very mean.
So mean they made me want to scream.
The suffering is awful and it's everywhere.
I kept asking myself, why doesn't anyone
care?

"Life on the streets is hard to take.
It certainly isn't a piece of cake.
You learn how to beg and then how to steal
if they're the only means of getting a meal.

"When it's bitter cold or there's sleet and rain,
you feel certain you can't bear the awful pain.
You search and search trying to find
a place where you'll find some piece of mind.

"Many homeless die from the bitter cold.
Some are young and some are old.
And when it's hot and very dry
we all search for water. Without it we'll die.

"Many die from the heat of summer.
Living on the streets sure is a bummer.
When you're feeling hopeless and there's
no place to hide,
you wish you had a friend close by your side,
someone who'll tell you it'll be okay,
that things will be better on the following day.

"Then one day a man in a van stopped by.
He got out, walked towards me and shouted Hi!'
I knew he was from a place that's called a pound.
It's sort of an animal lost and found.

"But if someone doesn't come by and adopt you
soon, in a few weeks or perhaps a month or two,
then you're time probably is up and the end is near.
This is what non human inmates have to fear.
So I ran and hid until he drove away.
I cannot forget him or that scary day.

"I met other dogs and lots of cats too.
They lived on the streets in the summer heat,
in the winter too when it was bitter cold.
As I told you before, some were young and some were old.

"Some stopped breathing from the cold and heat.
Some because they had nothing to drink or eat.
Some were killed by cars and trucks.
"Sometimes I saw it happen. I watched them die.
Then I'd start to cry and again ask, 'Why?'
Why, oh why, did they have to die?"

Chapter Sixteen

Becoming and Being Homeless, According to Murphy

"Losing a job can lead to losing a home
and everything else you once called your own.
Some have family who can give them some money.
But the money doesn't last. Being poor sure
isn't funny.

"No matter how hard the homeless try,
it is hard for them to understand why
the place which once was their home,
the place, which for years, was their very own,
                              no longer is.
                              no longer is.

"Becoming homeless can happen to anyone:
to children, the elderly and those in between.
It crosses boundaries and species too,
and it matters not if you have four feet or two.
This terrible thing can happen to you
                              or to someone you love,
                              or to someone you know,
                              or to any someone.

"When you're living on the streets and are all alone
it is hard to believe you once had a home.
But there are some who never had a home of their own.
I don't know which is worse. Both are bad.
Being homeless sure is very sad.
Being homeless sure makes one very sad.

"And it doesn't matter if you have four feet or two.
Life on the streets is not good for you
                          or for someone you love,
                          or for someone you know,
                          or for any someone.

"You won't understand it unless you've been there.
Just ask the homeless. They're everywhere!
I suppose that's how it was for me.
I didn't understand until it happened to me.

"Then one day when I was feeling real bad,
I mean helpless and hopeless and very sad,
I saw that same man pull up in his van.

"I was filled with despair. Why didn't anyone care?
I felt I'd been cheated. I felt defeated.
Nobody cared and I was filled with despair.
So this time I didn't run or hide.
I walked over to the man and stood by his side.

"He brought me to a shelter that's called a pound.
As I explained before, it's a kind of lost and found.
And just before my time was up
I got lucky! Real lucky!! Really Lucky!!!
Greta arrived and adopted me!

"Then like magic my life changed for the better.
I went to a comfortable home and lived with Greta.

Chapter Seventeen

Animal Research: It Hurts Everyone

"Shayna, you and I run very fast.
The two of us together have a blast.
Our fun takes place in a very safe yard
where Greta stands by just like a guard.

"She never leaves us outside alone.
She fears someone might grab us and steal us
from home.
It happens to lots of dogs and cats.
Some end up in a research lab.

"Those labs are bad. They're very bad.
Terrible things happen in a research lab.
The stolen victims are put in a crate
and suffering and torture become their fate.

"While living on the streets I met a dog.
He had been rescued from a research lab.
His rescuer loved him and treated him well.
He tried to make him forget his former life in hell.

"His name was Tim and he could barely speak,"
Murphy said and let out a sigh.
Murphy's tail went down and he tried not to cry.
"I could barely hear him," Murphy said in a whisper.
"I could barely hear him. Poor Tim. Poor Tim."

Shayna:
"Greta, how could this have happened to him?
How could this have happened to poor, sweet Tim?"

Greta:
"In the laboratory they cut his vocal chords."

"But why did they cut his vocal chords?"

"So no one would hear him when he was crying in pain
because of the terrible things they did to him.
So no one would hear him while he was dying in pain because
of the cruel, senseless things they did to him.
In a research lab.

"Vivisection is torture; it isn't right.
Its victims are helpless and unable to fight.
They cannot protect themselves from this terrible blight.
Animal research is a terrible disgrace.
It makes you wonder about the human race.

"Torturing animals and putting them through hell
have nothing to do with making people well.
But even if it did, it still would be wrong
to torture and kill them to make humans strong.

"There are differences between humans who are
young and old
and between men and women, so I am told.
There are differences between dogs and cats.
The same is even true of mice and rats."

Shayna:
"If the differences are even greater between humans
and us,
animal research should be banned without any fuss."

Greta:
"You're right, Shayna.
Experimenting on animals is all about money.
It doesn't help people and the results aren't funny.
It's painful and deadly to you and to us.
It should be banned Now without any fuss."

Murphy:
"Now I understand the awful things they did to Tim.
They should not have done those terrible things to him!"

"Murphy and Shayna, I'm so proud of you.
You understand more than most people do.
Yes, testing on animals is Deadly Nonsense."
It's been proven that such testing is lethal and
useless.
It should be banned Now without any fuss!"

The following are some of many signs the author read while participating in some peaceful protests against animal testing/vivisection:

VIVISECTION: Science Gone Mad!

A Lab Animal Never Has a Nice Day.

Torturing Animals Doesn't Cure Humans.

Animals Are Not ours to Eat, Wear, Experiment On or Use in Entertainment.

Many, many thousands of former racers have been and continue to be sold by trainers to research labs and some veterinary colleges where they undergo painful experiments and then are killed.

According to Physicians Committee for Responsible Medicine (PCRM.org):

"Each year, more than 8,500 goats and pigs are used in combat trauma training courses conducted for U.S. military personnel. In many of the courses, animals are shot or stabbed or their limbs are amputated in an attempt to mimic battlefield wounds. At the end of the course, the trainees kill their wounded animal patients. This trauma training is conducted on as many as 15 U.S. military facilities, including Fort Bragg and Fort Sam Houston, as well as in facilities run by private contractors."

Personal Comment:

Try to imagine what this killing does to these medical trainees from a psychological perspective. This murder continues even though there are simulators that are like human bodies and are much more effective than the torturing and murdering of live animals.

Vivisection/animal experimentation is a multi million dollar industry that benefits only the murderers in white coats and their CEOs.

Chapter Eighteen

More about the Language Dogs
Use to Speak and Communicate

Sometimes when Greta was watching TV,
Shayna walked over in order to see
what was going on in that big, old box.
"Nothing," she'd say, "that's of interest to me."

"Greta, please get up and play with me.
If you don't, here's what I'm going to do:
I'm going to bark and shriek and bother you."

As for Murphy, when Greta was watching TV,
he barked very loud, which meant, "Oh Gee,
come on over and play with me
instead of watching that old TV."

Murphy discussed this with Shayna and then he said.
"No more TV. No siree!
No more TV. None at all.
Not when the three of us could be having a ball."

Greta got up and shut off the TV.
"Okay you two, what shall it be?
C'mon you two, what do you say?
Tell me what you want to play."
And they told her!
At other times Murphy would bark

"Turn off the TV. Come on over and talk to me.
Talking is just as important as playing.
There are so many things I want to be saying
to you.

"We don't believe we're being unfair
when we ask you to listen and be aware
of what we're trying to say to you.
So listen to us. Please do! Please do!"

And Greta listened.

"Our barks may sound rather strange to you.
Peoples' words often sound strange to us too,
But we don't laugh and make fun of you.
So we expect respect from people too."

"Some barks," said Shayna, "mean we want to play
or go for a walk or sit and talk.
Other barks mean we're feeling glad, real glad.
Still others mean we're feeling depressed or scared.

"Soft whines can tell you something too.
They're our way of saying, we're here and we need you.

"Watch our eyes," continued Shayna, "they tell you
so much.
They tell you as much as a kiss or a touch.
To gain entry to our souls, watch our eyes.
They speak the truth. They don't speak lies."

"Our tails," said Murphy, "tell you something too.
They can give you an important clue or two.
Down means we're feeling bad,
something's not right; we're feeling sick or scared.
Up and wagging means we're feeling just fine
and we want to talk or walk if you have the time."

"Murphy and Shayna, you're so very smart.
Most humans don't know it or don't want to
admit it.
They prefer to believe you're not as smart as they are.
They prefer to believe you're even less than they are.
This is what people have said for years and years.
For those who aren't human it must stir up fears."

"It does" said Shayna, "and it certainly isn't true
that we are not as smart and are less than you.
Since we try so hard to understand humans,
they should try to understand us too."

Once again Greta spoke:

"Let us consider whales and dolphins and elephants too.
We can't hear the sounds they use to talk to one another.
Does that mean they do not communicate?
Absolutely not! Absolutely not!
They speak! They speak! They speak to one another!
They communicate!

58

"As for bears, lions, tigers and other wild ones,
their growls and other sounds have meaning too.
Those sounds are not noise! They are not noise!
Please remember this, girls and boys!
Those sounds are their means of communicating."

Chapter Nineteen

The Happier Times When Life Got Better Once Murphy and Shayna Started Living with Greta

One day I heard Greta say,
her voice full of laughter, love and play,
"go get the toy you handsome boy."

She threw a toy across the room.
Murphy chased it and when he came near,
it bounced and pounced and landed on his ear.

This didn't scare him and he tells us why:
"the bouncer is my favorite toy."
Murphy then smiled and breathed a joyful sigh.

"Go get the whirl, you adorable girl."
What is a whirl? Why, it's a ball with a curl.
When you throw it, it doesn't bounce up and
down.
Instead, it makes all kinds of faces ----
happy ones, silly ones and ones with a frown.
Some faces looked joyous and some looked sad.
Some looked silly and some even looked mad.

Shayna pounced on the whirl with all her might.
Murphy did too and they had a fun fight
that lasted for a minute and sometimes more.
Then they'd both flop down exhausted on the floor.
It was so much fun having fun.

Murphy was agile and could jump very high.
Why, he jumped so high he almost reached the sky.
Or so it seemed.
He'd jump over and over and over and then
jumped again and again and again.

"Whenever I jump I feel so free.
Whenever I jump I'm glad I'm me."

One day Greta saw her shoes on the bed.
Again!
There was a frown on her face and to Shayna she said,
"Please put them back. Please do! Please do!"
But Shayna shook her head and said, "No! No!"
She refused to budge. She sat and sat.
She shook her head, which meant, "That's that!"

"Shayna," said Greta, "please don't be a pest.
Are you trying to put me through some kind of test
to see if I love you? You know I do.
You know that I love the two of you
So very much! So very much!"

"Greta," said Shayna, "it isn't a test
to see if you love me. I know you do.
This is one of my ways of having fun.
Murphy's not the only one who likes to have fun.
I do too."

So Shayna continued being silly.
"Murphy, Murphy, oh well, well, well!
Go and ring the ding dong bell."

"Shayna," said Murphy, "stop being so silly.
You're talking like a willy- nilly."

"I like to be silly and have some fun
with you or Greta or anyone,"
Shayna replied with a silly smirk.
Yes, that Greyhound sure was some piece of work!

"Shayna, Shayna, No! No! No!
Your silliness has got to go."

"Murphy, stop being such a grouchy grouch!
Go take a nap on our new couch.
Greta won't mind, not one bit,
whereas other humans probably
would have a fit."

Then Greta said to Murphy, "My handsome boy,
I thank you for bringing me so much joy.
And precious Shayna, so funny and sweet,
I'm grateful that we three did meet.

"Often when I'm feeling down and blue,
my spirits rise just thinking about you.
I love you both with all my being.
You've given my life so much meaning."

Chapter Twenty
Conclusion

"Greta, Greta," Shayna said,
I like to lie close to you on the bed.
I like to rest my head upon your shoulder.
I'll do it until we all grow much older,
until I no longer can jump on the bed.
That will be an unhappy day,"
pretty Shayna very quietly said.

"When that day comes we'll cut down the bed
and you'll always be able to get on the bed.
So have no fear, Shayna dear," Greta said.
Shayna smiled and moved closer to Greta.
She felt safe and content. She never felt better.

"What are the two of you doing in there?
To leave me out is just not fair.
I'm important! I count too!
What you do for Shayna you should do for me too."

"Murphy, Murphy, come over here.
I love you too. Never fear.
Even death won't make us part because
it's only our physical bodies that die
while our spirits/souls soar to the heavens and sky.

"So jump on the bed and snuggle with us.
Snuggle with us without any fuss."

And Murphy did.
"I'll never love anyone more than you two;
perhaps just as much, but never more."
Murphy was happy and jumped back onto the floor.

The three of them played often, sometimes on the floor.
They gave each other hugs and kisses galore.

A few weeks later
Murphy and Shayna went for a ride.
Murphy then asked Shayna to be his bride.
"Yes, yes, Murphy, yes my dear.
Let's get married sometime this year."

And guess what? They did!

More about Us

"We have 2 horses and a calf living with us.
Greta rescued them without any fuss.
We also have three cats in our barn.
They once were homeless but no longer are.
They are safe living here and will never ever
come to harm.

Both horses love our calf whose name is Minh.
Baron is especially protective of him."

The Feelings and Thoughts of Homeless Dogs and Cats that Murphy Heard While Living On the Mean Streets

I'm hungry. I'm starving.
I'm cold. I'm freezing.
I'm so hot I can't breathe.
I'm so thirsty I can't swallow.
I'm hurting. I'm frightened
I'm sick. I'm scared.
I can't stop crying.
I think I'm dying.
I'm pregnant. Oh Gee!
Why didn't somebody spay me?

Epilogue

If there were no homeless dogs and cats,
or humans and other animals, including rats,
What a wonderful world this would be!

If all living creatures had a home,
a place they could call their very own,
What a wonderful world this would be!

If everyone had enough to eat
and were strong enough to stand on their feet,
Oh, what a wonderful world this would be!

Food isn't scarce. There's plenty around.
It just must be moved to wherever
it is needed the most.

Some countries have plenty of food to spare.
The problem is getting it moved to where
it is desperately needed, needed the most.

If all of this could just be done,
a life-saving battle would be won and
What a wonderful world this would be!
Oh, what a wonderful world this would be!

If all living beings were treated as worthy,
if all species were respected and none were rejected,
What a wonderful world this would be!
Oh, what a wonderful world this would be!

If cruelty to others became a thing of the past,
if vivisection was outlawed and very fast,
if hunters stopped hunting and said, "No More!"
If slaughter houses everywhere shut down forever
once their owners became enlightened and said,
"What for? What for?
What a wonderful world this would be!
Oh, what a wonderful world this would be!

If one day some government called a war
and good people everywhere said, "No More!
What for?"
And if nobody came! If nobody came!
What a wonderful world this would be!
Oh, what a wonderful world this would be!

Additional Information

Shayna is the Greyhound responsible for the banning of dog racing in Massachusetts. It was a difficult 17 year battle. My precious girl passed away from bone cancer during the campaign in October, 1998 when she was just ten and one half years of age. Murphy passed in January 2000. He was between 11 and 12 years of age. These were heartbreaking losses as are all of our losses. The dog racing ban finally was passed in November 2008.

While working on one of the bills to ban dog racing in MA in 1998 (three were filed but none were ever reported out of committee), I noticed that Shayna was limping. I was scared. I was terrified that it might be a sign of bone cancer. This disease has killed and continues to kill so many racers and former racers. I brought her to the veterinarian the next day, she brought Shayna into the x ray room and when she returned she was crying. Shayna had bone cancer. Three weeks later she was gone. I didn't think I could go on without her. It was a struggle, a struggle for Murphy too. I didn't think I'd make it. But I did, with Murphy at my side. A couple of months later Diana came into our lives. More about her later.

Shayna was adopted from Greyhound Friends in Hopkinton, Massachusetts. She was found in a local cemetery, she was wearing a racing muzzle and was quite emaciated. She was rescued by an animal control officer who brought her to Greyhound Friends. Her story can be read in a book I wrote called "The Story of My Life, by Shayna, as told to Greta."

We do not know how Shayna ended up in a cemetery. We do know that sometimes when a racer no longer is profitable he or she is abandoned. This might have happened to Shayna. We do not know. We do know that when she finally was rescued by a caring animal control officer, this lovely former athlete was near death from the elements, starvation and dehydration.

I adopted Murphy after reading an ad in a local newspaper in 1989 or 1990. It said "Please Help! Home desperately needed for a teddy bear of a dog." He had been found wandering the streets. After reading the ad I called the shelter while I was at work and told them I'd pick him up on the way home from work. I was a probation officer and lived not far from where the shelter was located. I took Murphy home with me that very same day. This was shortly after the passing of Pumkin and Minh, two adorable pugs. After living with these little ones for about thirteen and fourteen years, I thought Murphy, who weighed about 60 pounds, looked like a giant.

Murphy's and Shayna's story was slightly edited again in February 2014 in Easthampton, MA. Since the previous editing in April 2003, many cherished four legged ones have entered and left my life. They now are cherished spirit angels. J.J. is one of them. He was a Greyhound who never raced. He was twelve years old and in desperate need of a new home. We welcomed him into our home. He was sweet and gentle and became Murphy's and Shayna's dear friend. I referred to him as our elder statesman. He passed away at age fourteen.

Other spirit angels include sweet and precious Diana; funny and precious Danny Boy whom I named after one of my favorite songs. When he passed away at age ten from bone cancer I no longer could play Danny Boy on my guitar. I just couldn't.

Danny Boy was a handsome black Greyhound. When he first entered my life he did not trust people and felt more relaxed when visitors would sit down near him and talk to him. He gradually became a funny and happy, adorable guy.

I adopted Diana shortly after Shayna's passing. I visited a Greyhound adoption group. Looking at all of the beautiful dogs I asked who had been there longest. Someone pointed at a lovely, black female and said she was. I said I'd take her. Her racing name was Nosey Nora. Yes, Nosey Nora! I changed it to Diana because I had seen many pictures of the Goddess Diana with a Greyhound at her side. Many months later I learned that Diana was the goddess of hunting! Oh well!!

She and Murphy became good friends, although not as close as Murphy and Shayna had been. After Murphy was diagnosed with melanoma and lay dying, Diana never left his side except when she ate or went outside to relieve herself. It was two days before the veterinarian arrived and released Murphy. Diana then developed a severe case of diarrhea, so severe that it lasted more than a week and required a change in her diet. This did not surprise me or the veterinarian. Murphy passed away about fourteen months after Shayna's passing. Now the two good friends are together again.

Danny Boy entered our lives when he was about six years old. He was a big and handsome black Greyhound. He was a beauty. As already noted, I named him Danny Boy after my favorite song. He had quite a personality, especially when he wanted my attention. One day in early May 2005, I noticed that he was limping. An x ray of his leg was negative. Yet I felt lots of anxiety. Lots! Three weeks later he was still limping and a second x ray revealed bone cancer. That is how I lost my Danny Boy. He was ten years old and I loved him so much.

One month later, in July 2005, a nine and one half year old Greyhound entered our lives. I named him Papa Frankie, after my very special and much cherished father. Papa Frankie didn't stay with us very long. One morning he and I and two other Greyhounds were in our back yard. They were having fun. When we went back into the house he bumped into an empty card board carton and started to scream. He too had bone cancer and joined Danny boy less than two years after Danny Boy's departure. Loving can be so painful.

Tommy was another very special Greyhound (they all are special) who, at three years of age, developed seizures while racing on the track and who tragically, oh so tragically, passed away at age seven and one half years of age. He left so young in spite of the excellent care he received from me and the wonderful veterinarians and persons at Northampton Veterinarian Clinic in Northampton, MA.

Lucky was an adorable and oh, so funny Dalmatian. He was a rescue who entered our lives when he was past ten years of age and left us three and one half years later. Lucky and Tommy were very close friends, perhaps because they both were so fun-loving and full of mischief. Often when I was seated at the kitchen counter eating a sandwich, the two of them would appear and one of them would grab the sandwich out of my hand and run off with it. They were partners in mischief, so adorable and writing about them brings smiles and tears to my face. As already noted, Lucky passed away three and one half years after entering our lives. He was fourteen or almost fourteen. Tommy left us just two months later. As already noted, he was just seven and one half years of age. Loving sure can be painful.

Finally there was my sweet Danielle. Danielle was a former racer whom I adopted at age eight. After Diana left us I told a friend, Robin that I wanted to adopt a Greyhound who was in desperate need. Robin knew who to call. She called a rescuer in Florida (Joey's Greyhound Friends) and explained what I had requested. Brigitte Cooper, a Greyhound rescuer, told Robin she knew of a dog whose racing days were long over. She had been used as a brood momma who had just one litter of puppies and could have no more. She now was being very sorely neglected, if not worse.

Brigitte had recently rescued several older, needy girls from a Florida track and was upset because she had no more room in her kennel or her house to rescue another dog. Arrangements were made to have this Greyhound transported to a wonderful group, Greyhound Options, in Ware, MA. This is how Danielle entered our lives. When she first arrived, her tail was touching her belly, her body was shaking and she barked constantly.

One day my recently adopted five year old granddaughter was visiting. She is an inter racial child whose previous life had been pretty horrific. She asked why Danielle was barking. I explained that Danielle was afraid of people. People had abused her. My granddaughter replied, "Me too."

It took many months and lots of love before Danielle's tail relaxed and the trembling and barking stopped. As her stress lessened, Danielle became gentle and loving. She accepted Tommy and Lucky when they entered our lives and the three of them would lie on my bed at bed time. After they passed away she accepted Mr. White, my present earth angel. Danielle was loving and gentle. In spite of her sad and unhealthy past, she lived for fifteen years and two weeks. She was my miracle girl, my gorgeously adorable girl and Mr. White's dear friend. Unfortunately, my lovely granddaughter, she now is fifteen, has not fully recovered from her brutal, abusive past.

A Spiritual Encounter:

Danielle was released at about 5 P.M. on Thursday, February 9, 2012. Although I have been experiencing insomnia for many years, that night I fell asleep with no trouble. Strange. Sometime in the very late hours of the night or the very early hours of the next morning – it was very dark, I suddenly awoke. I sat up in my bed, my eyes wide open. I looked to my right, and there was a vision of my Danielle. She was standing about a foot away from me looking tall, dark and gorgeous. The vision lasted about 15 seconds and then she disappeared.

Again I fell asleep immediately and when I awoke in the morning I was filled with joy. So much joy! My precious Danielle was alive and well. Yes, her physical body had died, but she had not and I have never grieved over my precious girl.

Then God put the greyhound on earth
to live among men and to remember.
And when the time comes God will call
the greyhound back to paradise to testify
about men and God will judge accordingly.

old Persian proverb

I must also acknowledge a beloved cow named Minh, whom I rescued when he was three days old. After he finished drinking from his bottle he would suck on my forefinger for a few minutes. Baron, one of my horses, was very protective of him. Whenever a new horse arrived Baron would place himself between Minh and the new horse until he was certain that the latter would not harm Minh.

Baron was a former pacer who was retired to a good home after he was injured. He was one lucky horse! Most do not fare so gently. One day someone called me and advised that Baron needed a new home because his persons now were elderly and unable to provide proper care. I agreed to take him. When he arrived I was stunned. He was absolutely gorgeous! Handsome! Overweight too. About one hundred pounds! It was not a problem. Good hay, grass, clean water and just a small handful of grain. As he lost weight he became even more handsome and I felt a good deal of relief.

Baron eventually was adopted by the woman who adopted Brody. He and Brody became good friends and like Brody, Baron lived a long and good life. But it was so hard to let him go. So very hard. I loved him so much!

When Minh was about four years old I decided to move elsewhere because I could not get the help I needed caring for my large, four legged treasures. I was divorced and it was impossible to find decent and capable helpers. At the time, my rescues included two horses and Minh. I would not, however, put my house and barn up for sale until I found excellent homes for the three of them.

An animal rights organization suggested a sanctuary that would be an excellent home for Minh: Poplar Springs in Poolesville, Maryland. I contacted another organization and was told that Poplar Springs was an excellent choice. I called and spoke to Terry Cummings, co-founder of the sanctuary with her husband, Dave Hoerauf. I told her all about Minh and she said they were so new that Minh would be their first cow. At the time their residents consisted of 3 horses and some chickens. They drove to Lanesboro, met Minh, Murphy and Shayna and our 2 two resident horses. We talked, ate a delicious vegan lunch and got to know and like each other. After many, many hours they left, taking with them my precious guy.

We kept in touch. Terry told me that Minh was so very comfortable around horses. Of course he was. He had been raised with horses and Baron was his protector. Terry told me that when some cows finally arrived at the sanctuary Minh was confused. He was hesitant, uncertain. This is understandable. He was taken from his mother when he was just three days old. It took time, but eventually he felt comfortable in the company of other cows.

I visited Minh a few months later. There were no other persons in the barn. I did not see Minh so I sat down on the barn floor and called his name. Soon he came walking towards me, sat down next to me and put his head on my lap. I kissed my adorable guy. I loved him so much! I visited him again and again, once when he was in the woods. Terry drove me to a certain area. I got out of her vehicle, walked down a hill and called his name. Soon he was near me. I hugged him over and over and over again. When he had had enough he gently released himself from my arms and looked at me for several minutes, letting me know that he recognized me. He allowed me one more hug, then turned around and walked back into the woods.

Minh was about fourteen when Terry called me one morning. Minh had gone to sleep last night and not awakened. They were shocked! He had seemed so healthy! There had been no signs of illness! We were grief stricken. But he had not suffered and for that we were grateful. He now was in another and better dimension. Only his body had died. Of that I was certain. Still, the tears would not stop and I thought that my heart was breaking into bits and pieces. The numbers of my cherished spirit angels had increased again and I had to be strong. I had to be strong. What other choice was there?

Terry told me that visitors had loved Minh so much! He was friendly, gentle and full of mischief. When visitors arrived he'd greet them as they got out of their cars, then he'd reach into their cars and pull out packages, water bottles and more. He brought smiles to so many faces. They loved him so much, as did Terry, Dave and I. Now he and Baron are together again in that beautiful dimension that is invisible to human eyes. There were many more magical creatures: among them cats Rumpi (named after Rumplestiltskin), Sam and many other rescued felines of long ago who were adopted and named by their new guardians. Here is Sam's story.

It was the mid 1980s and I was living in Long Beach, N.Y. One day a cat appeared at my house and would not leave. She was not wearing a collar. After feeding her for a month or two outdoors, I brought her into the house. Pumkin and Minh, my two little pugs, did not object. Soon thereafter I brought her to a veterinary hospital and told the veterinarian that Samantha needed to be spayed. He examined her, smiled and told me that his name is Sam and he needed to be neutered. The two of us burst out laughing.

There were many more horses. Let me tell you Georgie Girl's story. Georgie Girl was given to me, via a third party, by racing people because she no longer could race. She severely damaged a leg while racing. Her racing name was pretty awful and so I renamed her Georgie Girl. I was stunned when, a month or two later, the veterinarian informed me that she was pregnant. I was stunned! If the racing people found out they surely would want the foal for racing purposes. This was not acceptable. We kept the birth a secret. Someone suggested we name the foal Secret Story. We did.

Then there were May and Snoopy. May was a former polo pony who no longer was a winner and was destined for slaughter. Snoopy had a misshapen front leg. He was rescued a day before the slaughter house truck was to take him away. His ridiculous name was changed by the nice lady who adopted him.

Joe Namath was another rescued horse, although he did not live with me after his rescue. I named him after Joe Namath, the football legend. A knowledgeable friend waited at the back of a race track. She knew that slaughter house trucks waited there to take away horses who had lost a few races and others who had suffered serious injuries while racing. Joe Namath, the man, was able to retire after suffering serious knee injuries. Joe Namath, a three year old horse, had suffered serious knee injuries, but if not for his rescue, his destiny would have been death by slaughter and dinner for humans. This is the fate of so many horses once their humans decide they no longer are profitable.

And then there was Gabriel, beloved of Elaine Nash. One morning in late 1996 I received a phone call from a friend who was a horse rescuer. She said she had just received a phone call advising her that a three month old colt was in immediate and serious danger. He would be going to auction (and probable death) that day if she did not arrive that day and buy/rescue him. There was a problem: Her trailer was not working. Did I have access to a trailer to rescue/purchase him and then bring him to her farm? They wanted money. Miraculously, I discovered that I had three hundred dollars in cash in a bureau drawer. She said they'd be satisfied with that amount.

I then called my friend, Elaine Nash, explained the situation, and together we drove to Palmer, MA, about a two hour drive. When we arrived we discovered that this little guy was living in a junk yard with broken down cars. He was eating the upholstery in one car. Nearby his mom lay dying.

It was a shattering experience, one that nourished my already doubtful feelings about the human species. Elaine wanted to keep him and my other friend did not object. We named this little guy Gabriel, after the angel Gabriel and my friend Erica's Greyhound. Erica found a battered and bruised Greyhound, a former racer, wandering the streets of Pownel, Vermont. This was when dog racing was still legal in Vermont and abandonment of former racers was not an uncommon occurrence.

Yes, we rescued Gabriel from the hands of Death when he was just three months of age. He was severely infested with lice and parasites and those unspeakable three months of neglect and abuse prevented him from living a healthy and long life. Gabriel passed away when he was just fourteen in spite of the best care and love that he received. He was Elaine's beloved and my cherished god child. Gabriel too is among the many spirit angels who are loved for eternity.

Present equine god children include Gabriella and Narishka who are being cared for superbly by Elaine Nash. Likewise Greta Girl who, along with so many, many other horses, is being wonderfully cared for by my dear friend Vicky Berry, cofounder of CNEER (Central New England Equine Rescue), located in West Brookfield, MA. In 2005, Vicky and her daughter, Betsy Johnson, cofounded CNEER.

Gabriella is a former premarin mare who was rescued by a woman with initially good intentions but who knew little or nothing about horses. She eventually became a collector. Unfortunately, this is not an isolated case. It happens often. Too often. The horses were so severely neglected that someone contacted the authorities and several were removed from her property. Gabriella was not among them. It was winter and she and the remaining horses were cold and hungry. She and the other horses, among them stallions, lived in a holding pen. Without any shelter from the wind, rain or snow!

Compassionate local people would drop off bales of hay to keep the horses from starving. Gabriella was constantly pregnant.

Once again the authorities were summoned. When they arrived they found a stallion tied to a tree. He was practically dead from starvation and the elements and had to be euthanized. A woman approached the authorities and asked if she could take Gabriella. They gave their consent and she took Gabriella home. She wanted her because her daughter wanted Gabriella's unborn foal. So many people want foals, not recognizing that foals grow into large adult horses who require and deserve lots and lots of good care and love.

After her foal was born Gabriella was severely neglected. She was so hungry that she started eating tree bark. The woman's husband wanted to shoot Gabriella because the trees were dying. An acquaintance of Elaine Nash told her about this mare who was in danger. Serious danger! Elaine contacted the woman and then she and a friend drove to Vermont, observed the struggling mare and then returned home. That night Elaine did not sleep. She could not sleep because she kept thinking about the mare.

The next day she and two friends drove to Vermont. The woman was more than eager to let the mare go and the mare, smelling and seeing the delicious bales of hay, walked eagerly onto the trailer. Her goal: that delicious hay! Once at home, Elaine discovered that Gabriella was infested with worms and had severely damaged hooves.

After several months of veterinary care and love from Elaine, Gabriella was in good health. Elaine then drove her to Central New England Equine Rescue (CNEER). A couple of months later, Vicky Berry, founder of CNEER and others observed that the mare was not content living at the Rescue. She became difficult to manage, so Elaine brought her back home. Today Gabriella is a healthy and beautiful horse. In fact, she is a remarkable horse who miraculously still has faith in the human species. Gabriella was rescued one month after Gabriel's passing and, as you may have guessed, she is named in honor of our precious, spirit angel.

Narishka was about ten years old when she entered Elaine Nash's life. Previously, a woman had bought her and her foal at an auction house in Allentown, PA. where killer trucks line up and load up to take horses to slaughter. When the woman no longer wanted Narishka she called Elaine and told her quite bluntly that she no longer wanted her. She asked Elaine to take her. She wanted the foal only. Elaine knew that if she refused, Narishka would end up in the same auction house. The woman wanted money, so the money was raised and Elaine brought Narishka home. Today she is a happy, healthy and very beautiful horse. She and Gabriella are good friends. Elaine describes her own journey with these two horses as "a triumphant journey of the soul."

Shiloh recently passed away. He was a boarder on Elaine's property and he and Gabriella were inseparable. His body is buried on Elaine's property and she advises that she frequently finds Gabriella lying on or very close to his grave.

Brody was the first horse I rescued. It was August 1992 and my exquisite barn had just been completed. At my request, a knowledgeable friend went to an auction to bid against the killers. We were lucky. She did. The cost was $700 plus $35 tax. Reminiscent of slavery? My then-husband named him Brody after Brody Mountain in Western Massachusetts, where we lived.

I was able to contact Brody's former person. I told her that I, via a friend, had out bid the killers by just fifty dollars. Fifty dollars! She was shocked. Really shocked! Like so many others she was unaware of the connection between auction and slaughter. This woman told me that Brody had won many ribbons as a show horse but had been bucking and kicking when she tried to ride him. "He did well at shows, but not at home," she said. "Others could ride him, but not I." From our phone conversations and the letters she wrote to me I truly believe that she loved Brody and meant him no harm. She simply "traded" him for another horse, unaware that death by slaughter might have been his destiny. Brody was a wonderful horse who eventually was adopted by a good woman. He lived a long (mid thirties) and contented life.

Vicky Berry (CNEER) wrote the following about some of her many rescues:

Eco Doce was going to slaughter while in foal when we rescued her. She came to us at just two years of age with three abscessed hooves and barely able to walk. She was mal nourished, dehydrated and in desperate need of a bath. The veterinarian was not sure she could deliver a healthy foal. We gave her good nourishing food, clean water and TLC to rekindle her faith in the human species. She delivered a healthy colt. Both of these beautiful horses have been adopted to loving families. We see miracles and Eco Doce and her colt, Rio, are two of them! We thank our donors for their support in rescuing these beautiful horses.

Please note: When Eco Doce first entered our lives her coat was gray with a brown tint. This was due to severe mal nutrition. As she became healthier her coat turned tannish –gray. Today her coat is a beautiful dappled white, the color of a healthy Lusitano, which she is.

Greta Girl came into the Rescue in 2010. She was starving to death in a backyard field. The neglect she suffered was not her person's intent. The man loved his three horses and knew he was developing Alzheimer's. He was paying someone to buy Greta Girl and the two other horses hay and grain and feed them. The person he entrusted to care for his horses pocketed the money. Consequently, one horse died, one was taken by the SPCA and the Rescue took the mare and named her Greta Girl.

O'Reilly, a Thoroughbred, was purchased at an auction where the only other bidder was a killer bidder. He has a tattoo on his body, indicating that he is a former racer. Giovanni is another horse who was saved when CNEER outbid the kill buyer at an auction. Lukah, aka Laka, was born on May 30, 2014. His mom is a little Halflinger mare who was rescued while on her way to slaughter. Her name is Whisper, but I (Vicky Berry) call her Mama.

Millie the Mini.
Millie was going to slaughter when we heard of her plight. We raised the money to take her in and rehab her little soul. She is a dream mini, never does a thing out of step. It took a while and a lot of patience, TLC and kindness to get her to this.

It should be obvious from the preceding information that horse slaughter is big business in the United States and most of the world.

Thank you, Vicky Berry and everyone at CNEER, for saving these wonderful horses and many, many more precious equines, and to Vicky for providing us with the above information.

In 2014 authorities removed several horses from a terrible cruelty situation. They were brought to a shelter. One of them was a pregnant mare whose baby was born in September. In December mommy and baby went to live at Poplar Springs Animal Sanctuary. The former is five or six years of age, the latter is one-year-old.

The following was written by Terry Cummings of Poplar Springs Animal Sanctuary in Poolesville, MD.
"Bella and Fiona – Rescued from Starvation"
"In December 2014 we took in two beautiful Quarterhorses, a mare and filly, from a terrible cruelty case in Montgomery County, MD. Seven horses had been seized by animal control

from a nearby farm where they had been severely starved, neglected and kept with inadequate shelter and water. They were in such bad condition that one of the horses died after being rescued. Bella, the mare, was so emaciated that even though she was due to foal in two months, it was not obvious that she was pregnant.

Her baby, Fiona, was born two months after their rescue, and was miraculously healthy and normal. Prosecution of the owner of these horses is still pending. When Bella was rescued her feet were very cracked and overgrown and her tail was so matted it had to be cut off. It was not known when she had last been groomed or had her hooves trimmed.

Today Bella and Fiona are the picture of health. They are fat and happy, galloping, grazing and playing on the 400 acres of pastures and woods with the other rescued horses and Gloria, the mule. Fiona is growing quickly, but is never far from her very attentive mom. They are enjoying their lives, and will be able to happily live together for the rest of their days."

And Allah took a Handful of Southerly Wind
Blew His Breath Over It
and
Created The Horse.

—Bedouin Legend

Horses are highly intelligent, sensitive and intuitive creatures. I believe that the ancient Greeks were among the first persons to realize how important horses are in the human healing process. Today it is known as Equine Therapy. Horses are just one species of non humans who help humans, young and old, heal from that which is hurting them. The hurting can be mental, physical or both. Veterans are among the recipients as are other persons who are victims of trauma and violence. Horses and other non humans are life savers. Yet what do they get in return? For many: Death. So many domesticated horses end up in slaughter houses when their humans no longer want them. And as already noted, BLM round-ups result in the killing of thousands of wild horses. Justice. Where is justice? Compassion. Where is compassion?

As I continue my writing, Mr. White, a former racer, is my one and only earth angel. He entered Danielle's and my life a couple of months after Tommy passed. His racing name was Whitey, which I considered most undignified. I therefore named him Mr. White in honor of Walter White, a long-time-ago prominent figure in the NAACP. Mr. White is standing by my side as I type this note. He is beige and white, was adopted sight unseen and when he arrived at my house I asked, "Is he a Greyhound or a Deer?" Truth is, he is both a Greyhound and very Dear.

As of this writing, Mr. White is almost nine years of age. He has a splint in one leg. He broke it while racing. He too has seizures. They started when he was about seven and he is getting the best care possible. He is doing well and I hope that he and I (I'm way up there in age) make it together for some solid years to come. We communicate using words/sounds and gestures. Like Diana and Danny Boy, Mr. White becomes impatient, very impatient when I'm busy at the computer. He too wants my attention and emits plenty of soft sounds to let me know that he wants my attention.

Before concluding I'm asking readers to contact their representative and two senators in Washington, D.C. and ask them to support and co-sponsor two bills that would outlaw horse slaughter in the U.S. and would stop the transportation of horses from the U.S. to other countries where they are slaughtered: at present Canada and Mexico. As of this writing the two bills that would accomplish this are S 541 and HR 1094. Please Contact these persons.

Thank you so much and I hope you enjoyed reading Murphy's and Shayna's story as much as I enjoyed writing it.

Greta
February 23, 2014

Some Statements to Consider:

*As long as there are slaughter houses,
there will be battle fields.*
—Leo Tolstoy

*It is only a step from the murder of animals to the murder
of humans and thus also from the torture of animals to
the torture of humans.*
—Leo Tolstoy

*Where animals are concerned, everyone becomes a Nazi… every
day is Treblinka for the animals.*
—Isaac Bashevis Singer

*For some time he had been thinking of becoming a vegetarian.
At every opportunity he pointed out that what the Naziz did
with the Jews is the same as what people do to animals.*
—Isaac Bashevis Singer

*Auschwitiz begins whenever someone looks at a slaughter house
and thinks : they're only animals.*
—Theodore Adorno
Jewish man who fled the Nazis in 1939

As long as man massacres animals, they will kill each other.
—Pythagarous

Flesh eating is unprovoked murder.
—Benjamin Franklin

Whoever saves a single life is as if one saves the entire world.
—Talmud

For hundreds of thousands of years the stew in the pot
has brewed hatred and resentment that is difficult to stop.
If you wish to know why there are disasters of armies and
weapons in the world Listen to the piteous cries from the
slaughterhouse at midnight.
—Ancient Chinese Verse

The time will come when men such as I will look upon the
murder of animals as they now look upon the murder of men.
—Leonardo da Vinci

A Personal Comment:

Unfortunately, it appears that humans now look upon the murder of other humans as they look upon the murder of animals (non human animals). Once upon a time there were occasional brutal happenings called wars. Today they are every day brutal happenings. In addition, children are being taught to murder adults and other children. They are called child soldiers and are as young as eight years of age. Mr. da Vinci, I am sorry, so very, very sorry that your hopeful wish never materialized.

Slightly edited again in October 2015, at which time my handsome guy is ten and one half years of age. He is serene, gentle and loving and I want him to know:

Mr. White, my precious boy,
I thank you for bringing me so much joy.

Mr. White, oh Mr. White
I love you so, with all my might.

Mr. White, oh Mr. White,
you are my precious heart's delight.

Mr. White, you are my treasure.
You are someone I shall love forever
and ever and ever --------

The End!
Really! There's no more!
This is the End!

Murphy, one of Greta's Treasures and Shayna's best friend.

Murphy, Aug 28, 1993.

Shayna 1994.

Murphy in Shayna's bed.

Shayna in her bed.

Murphy, Shayna, Greta and Baron (the horse) in the barn.

Jay Jay aka J J (our elder statesman) Entered our lives at age 12, passed away at age 14 + 2 months.

Diana, soon after her rescue in Nov. 1998.
The bald spot was caused by living in a very small cage while she was still racing.

Several months after her rescue, Diana.

Diana and Greta's daughter Terri.

Diana lying at Murphy's side during the last two days of his life.

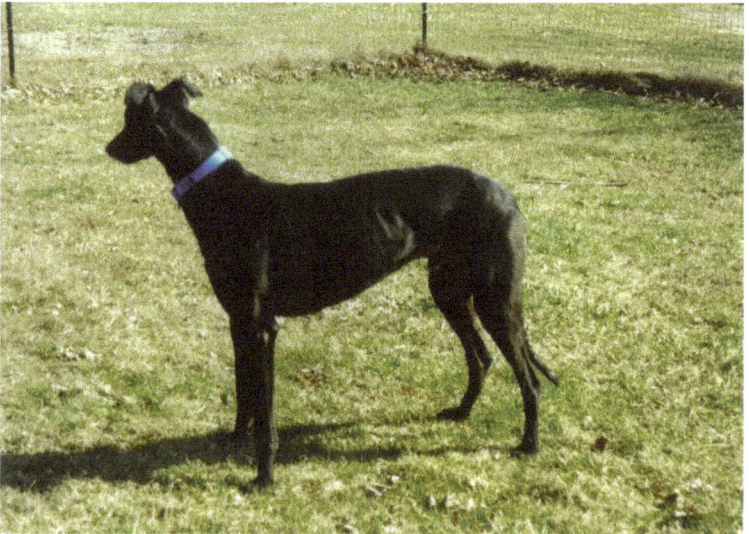

Danny Boy.

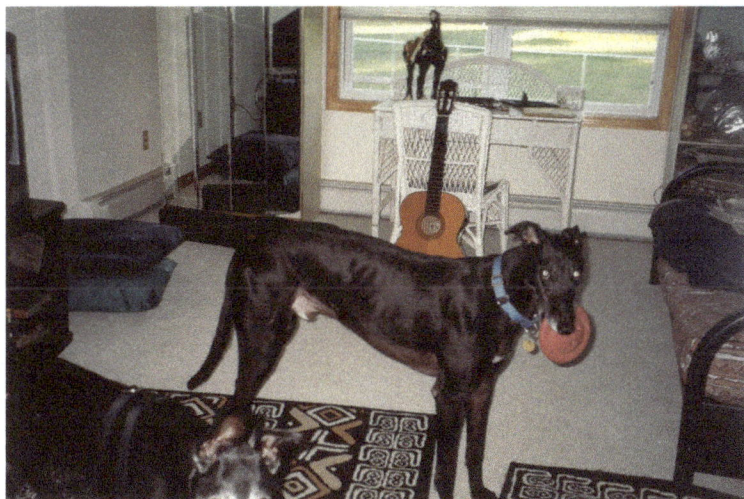

Danny Boy and his toy.

Diana and Danny Boy.

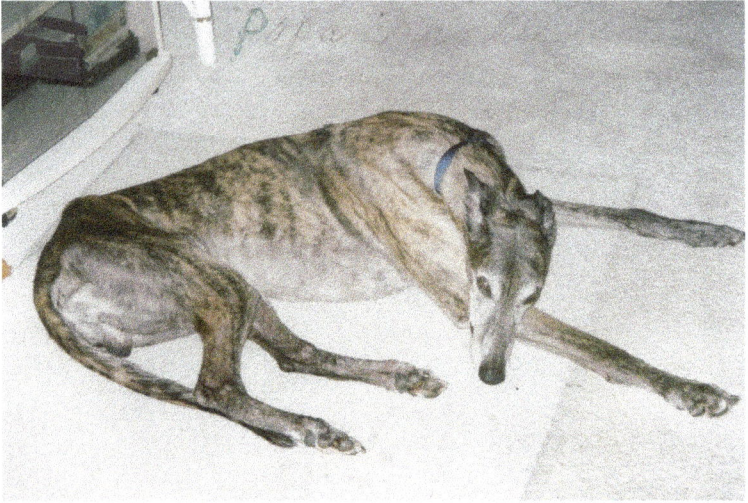

Papa Frankie, Summer 2005.

Dannielle, former racer miraculously lived to be 15 years old.
(plus 2 weeks)

Tommy on our bed. He was loving, fun-loving and full of mischief.
He left us much too soon. His body died but Tommy will live forever.

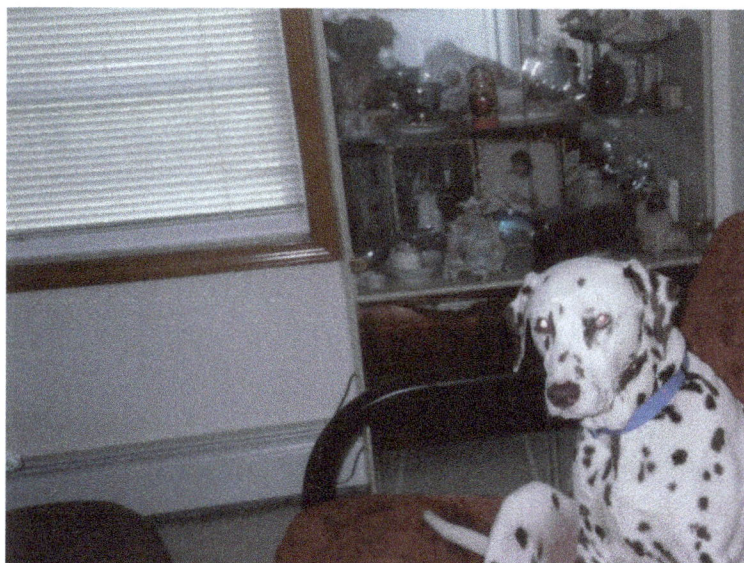

Lucky – Tommy's partner in mischief.

The four of us.

Two rescued cats.

Minh, a few days old.

Minh, a few days old.

Friend Matt Kelly and Minh at six months of age.
Matt and his wife Mary have rescued many non humans from slaughter,
especially turkeys and other birds; also a calf they named Albert. I
took care of Albert until they found a wonderful home for him.

Baron and Minh.

Baron and Minh.

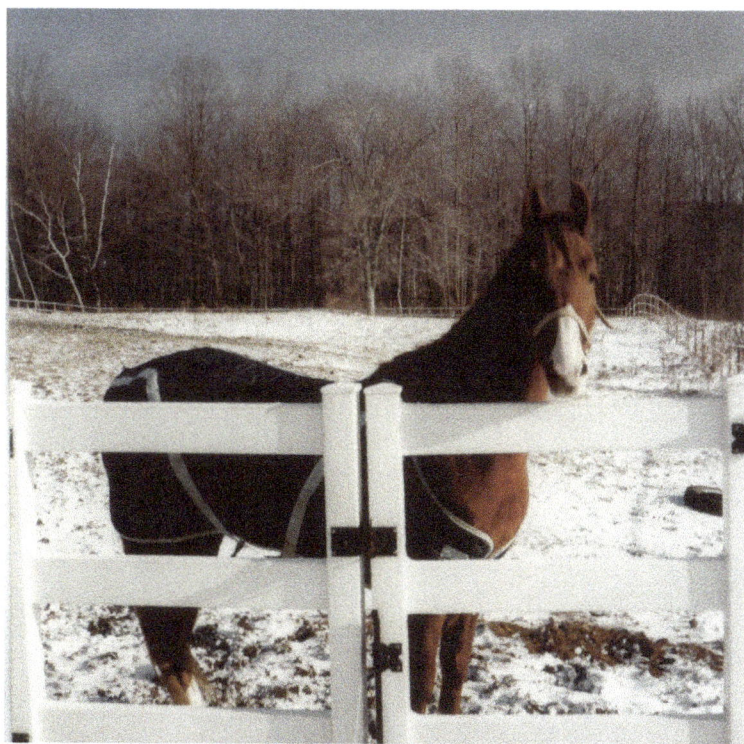

Brody (Greta's first rescued horse)

Brody (Again)

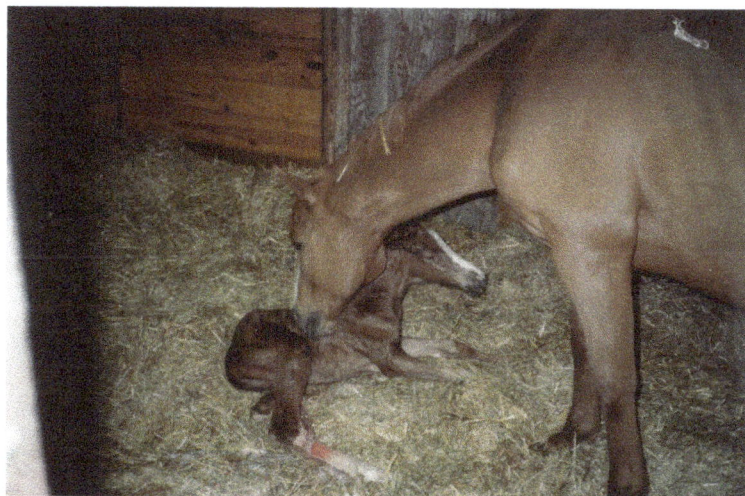

Georgie Girl and Secret Story.

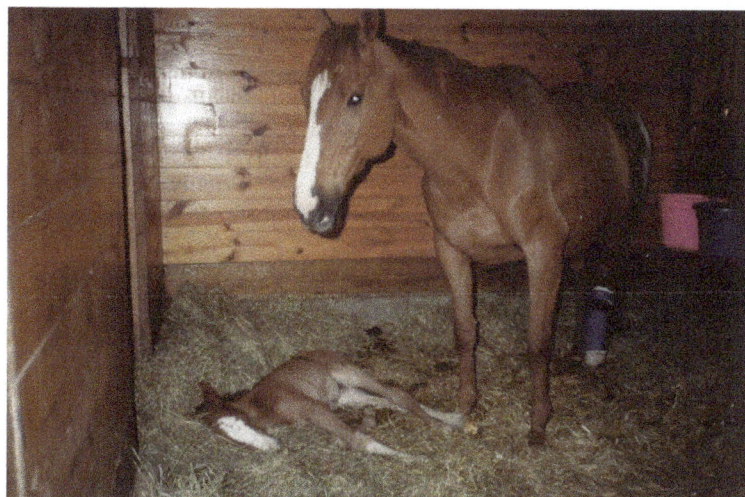

Georgie Girl and Secret Story.

Greta and Secret Story (Georgie Girl's baby)

Georgie Girl and Secret Story.

Gabriel (beloved of Greta and Elaine) shortly after his rescue.
Fake Fur.

Gabriel and Spatz (another one of Elaine's resues)

Gabriel and Spatz.

Greta's grandaughter Holly with Spatz.

Gabriella and Elaine Nash.
Former premarin mare.

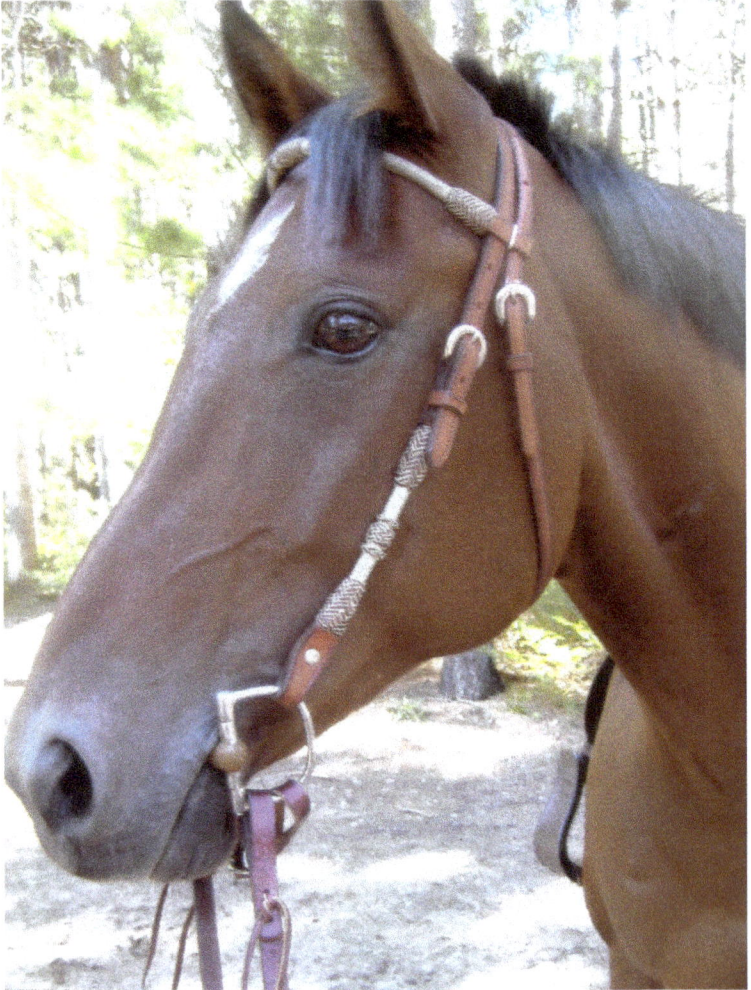

Gabriella.

Gabriella.

Narishka, In the past: constantly bred for monetary gain..
Today: A lovable horse, a joy to behold.

Narishka 2015.

Narishka 2015.

Elaine Nash and two goats she rescued at a petting zoo in Western Masachusetts. Most parents and children do not know that when petting zoos close in the fall , most of the animals go to auction, where they are sold for meat or canned hunts.

Bella and Fiona, Poplar Spring Animal Sanctuary.

Whisper was rescued from slaughter. She was in foal and going to slaughter. She was beautiful Lukah's mom. Her nickname is Mama.

Lukah, colt of Whisper , taking in the sunshine.
Lukah means "Bringer of Light".

Lukah and Logan. Logan is a foal of a Premarin mare rescued by CNEER. No one knew Logan's mom and it is not known what became of her. She probably went to slaughter when she was no longer useful.

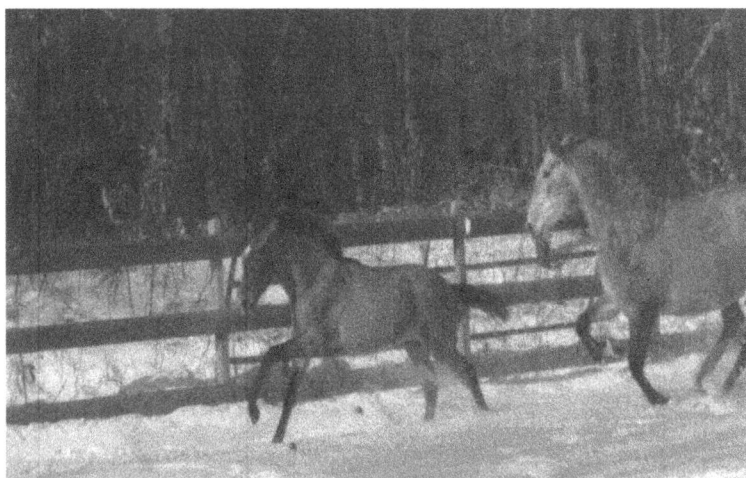

Eco Doce and her colt Rio. Eco Doce was going to slaughter while in foal when we rescued her. (CNEER)

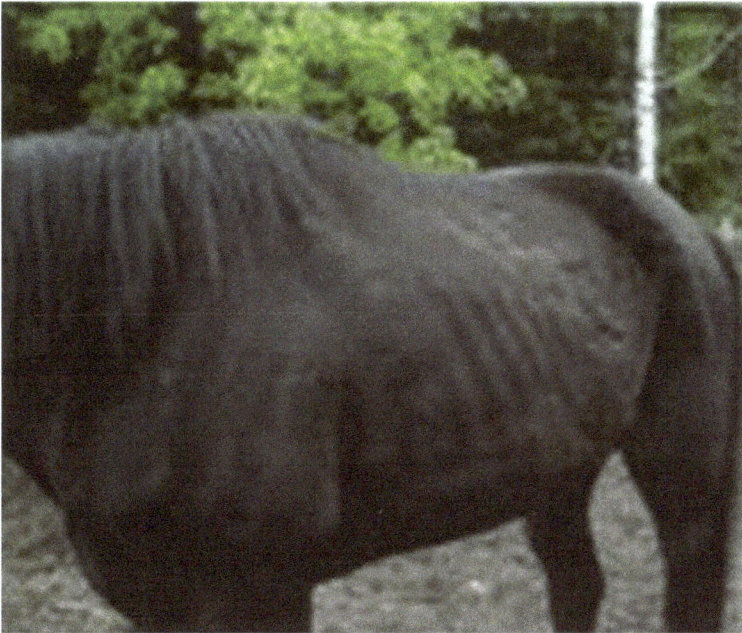

Giovanni when rescued from slaughter by CNEER.

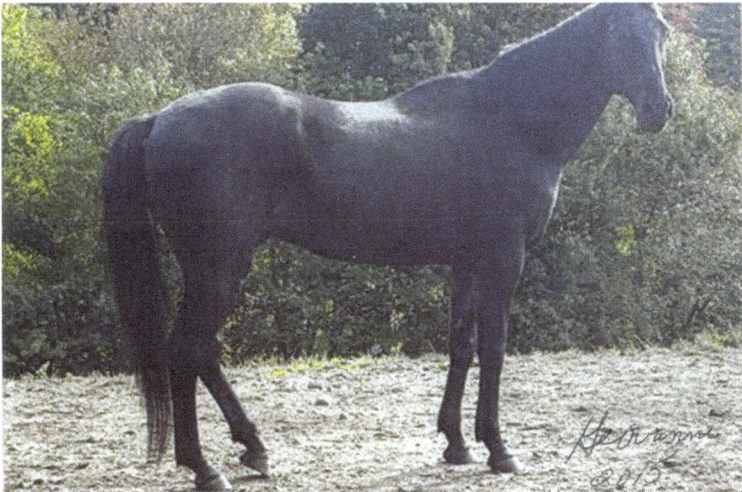

Giovanni – today 2015.

Greta Girl – before.

Greta Girl – after.

Greta and Jethro.
Greta was starving to death when we were asked to help. We could not
believe what we saw. She was skin and bone and her face was swollen
from infections. With care, good food, clean water and TLC Greta
came back to life and has been adopetd. Made a difference to this one.

Millie the mini. Millie was going to slaughter when we heard of her
plight. We raised the money to take her in and rehab her little soul. She
is a dream mini, never done anything out of step. It took a while and
lots of patience, TLC and kindness to get her to this.

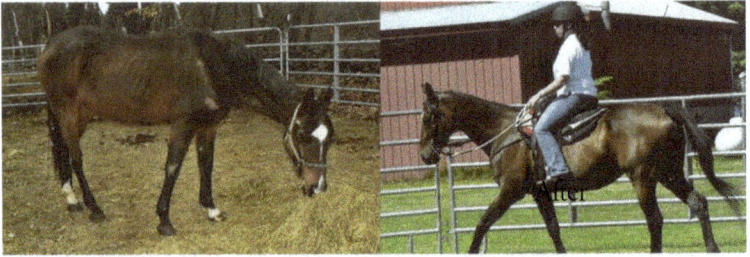

Before

After

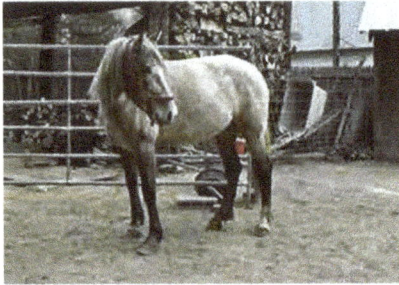

O'Rilley and Eco.

Joe Namath and co-rescuer Lisa

We Thank The Voters Of Massachusetts Who, In November 2008, Voted To End Dog Rac
In The Commonwealth. It Was A 17 Year Struggle That Finally Was Won.

Dog racing is not a sport.

It Is A Lethal Industry That Must Be Abolished
Nation-Wide! World-Wide! Likewise Horse Racing

Massachusetts Citizens Against Dog Racing.

Shayna
was found muzzled and starving in a Massachusetts Cemetery

VOTE YES ON
QUESTION 3

RACE CARS   NOT DOGS

FORMER RACER DIANA
&
RACE CAR DRIVER BILL KIRPENS SAY
RACE CARS NOT DOGS

Thank You

I Thank The Following Life-Saving Individuals and Organizations: Those already discussed in this book. Those not discussed in this book. Among them are four of my children.

Terri is a domestic and international human rights attorney who works to save the lives of innocent persons, here in the United States and abroad, especially in China. Falun Dafa is a form of religion similar to Buddhism. It was so popular in China that in the 1990s the Chinese Communist Party, a lethal dictatorship, outlawed the practice. Why? Because it was so popular that it frightened the CCP. In China Falun Dafa practitioners are kidnapped, arrested, tortured and murdered. In fact, many, many young and healthy practitioners have had and continue to have their vital organs removed (hearts, lungs, spleens etc) without benefit of anesthesia. The victims then are murdered (if they have not already died while under surgery) and their organs are sold world-wide to persons who need them.

Vicki is a licensed therapist who works primarily with people who have experienced trauma; ie; sexual, emotional and physical abuse. Her lovely adopted daughter has also been a victim of severe abuse. Vicki also adopted three Chihuahuas who desperately needed a good home. One of them, Jake, was killed in a tragic accident and I hope Vicki knows that it was only Jake' body that died. He never will die. Vicki is an exceptionally talented pianist and she and Joe, her former husband, have four amazing children: Meghan, Holly, Caitlin and Dylan. Joe is a fantastic guy and a great chiropractor. He is remarried to horse rescuer Abby, and we are all One Family. I must also acknowledge Holly's soon-to-be -husband Adam, a very special guy, and Dylan's cherished Fatima.

Michele is a child psychiatrist, a good one too! Her children, Margaret, Caroline and Alex are incredible persons. But then, so is their father John, a radiologist, who must share in the credit. Again, I must acknowledge Margaret's husband Adam, a very special guy, Caroline's dear friend Gabe and Alex's cherished Mary; also Margaret's and Adam's daughter, Greta. (the author's great-granddaughter)

Jonathan is an oncologist, a good one, who cares deeply about his patients. He and his wife Beth, do not have any 2 legged children together, but are the parents of three little pugs and two cats, all rescues. Sami, one of the cats, is blind in one eye.

Other outstanding individuals are Betsy Johnson, Bill Robinson, Carol Bishe, Ricco (Francis) Federico, Helen George and everyone else who is a part of Central New England Equine Rescue (CNEER). Special thanks to Betsy for rescuing/saving the lives of two precious calves.

Another outstanding individual is dear friend Alberto Gambarini, a retired neuro surgeon who, while practicing his profession, saved so many, many lives. As a student at a university in Argentina, his native country , he and other students protested when a Jewish professor was fired. He and the other students spent one month in jail. While celebrating the birth of the new state of Israel, he again was arrested and spent two days in jail. Alberto is a fantastic artist and is affectionately known as Tito.

Patrice and Kaare Bolgen, cherished friends. Kaare, now deceased, was a rare and wonderful person, a Norwegian who was active in anti-Nazi activities during World War II. He and Patrice were saving the lives of former racing Greyhounds (and other four legged ones) long before I got involved.

Joanne Hamilton and her remarkable family, Kim and Mark Bobrow. They have been rescuing four legged ones for many, many decades. Among them are horses, including a mini named Beau, dogs, cats, sheep, and chickens. Many are deceased, among them a little red hen named Henny. Goldie, Joanne's very first horse, healed her from that which was hurting her, hurting her terribly. She sometimes refers to him as her life- saver.

Erica Hartman, another cherished friend and Greyhound life-saver. While dog racing was still legal in Vermont, Erica rescued many abandoned Greyhounds who were wandering the streets not far from the dog track. Many were near death. Erica, who was not Jewish, was born and raised in Germany during World War II, married an American soldier, moved to the U.S. with him and made herself a promise to save lives whenever she could. She sure kept her word. My precious Erica no longer is among us. I know, however, that only her body died. Erica did not.

The anonymous man in the Massachusetts cemetery who phoned and begged an animal control officer to get to the cemetery as soon as possible to rescue an emaciated Greyhound who was in serious danger. Police had been summoned to get there and shoot her.

Ann, the animal control officer, who responded immedi-ately to the phone call, rescued the Greyhound and brought her to her shelter. She took excellent care of her for a few weeks until Greyhound Friends in Hopkinton, MA was able to take her. I've already thanked Louise Coleman and I thank her again.

Steve Madnick, my friend and former husband, now deceased, who insisted, yes, insisted that we adopt the exquisite new arrival. A few days earlier I had spoken to Louise who had suggested that I adopt Diane, who had been there for some time. But when Steve saw the beauty who had been rescued by the animal control officer, he was adamant. Louise was not present the day we arrived and when one of the volunteers heard the two of us arguing, she intervened. I told her that I had come for Diane and that the new arrival was so exquisite she would be adopted immediately. Diane had been there for some time. The woman assured me that they would find a loving home for Diane, that we should stop arguing and adopt the new arrival. Reluctantly, I agreed and named her Shayna, which means pretty in Yiddish. If not for Steve, Shayna would not have entered my life. It was Shayna's near-death experience in the cemetery that told me that dog racing must be banned. It now is banned in Massachusetts and several other states, but needs to be banned nation and world-wide. Horse racing and other forms of so-called "entertainment" also should be banned. Will they? What do you think?

My precious Shayna, the Greyhound behind the seventeen year struggle to ban dog racing in Massachusetts.

Shaun Kelly who, while a Massachusetts state rep in the 1990s, filed three bills to ban dog racing in MA. Not one of them made it out of committee. Shaun, you are a great guy and I think about you often.

Everyone who persevered on behalf of those three bills and then fought oh, so hard to ban this lethal industry via the ballot. Special thanks and so much love to Steve Baer, Libby Frattaroli and Robin Norton, Caroline Quinn and Karen Quinn. They were the first to join me and played a very vital role in achieving our goal. We are close friends to this day. I also thank Beverly Alba and all the other wonderful persons who worked on behalf of the dog racing ban. Incidentally, Steve adopted several rats who were rescued from a vivisection lab. I was aware that rats are very intelligent beings, but Steve informed me that they also are very loving creatures. In addition to participating in the dog racing ban, Beverly Alba also rescues many other four legged creatures.

Lisa De Mayo of Bonnie Lee Farm in MA, who, at my request, attended an auction and saved Brody from certain death. He was my very first horse rescue. Being a city person I knew little or nothing about horses and Lisa patiently taught me what I needed to know. Thanks, Lisa.

Other life- savers include dear friend and animal activist Beth Birnbaum who, as of this writing, is hospitalized for a serious brain injury. We do not know if she will make it. I love you Beth and I send thoughts of healing and love your way. It is good to know that her beloved cat, Mr. Chopinsky, is safe and in good hands.

Other life – saving persons/friends are Linda Gaunt, Jackie Gambarini (Massachusetts Voters For Animals and one of Tito's two very special daughters), Bill Haight, Linda Huebner, Corrine Martin, Sheila Milkowski, Batya Bauman, Sue Oppenheimer, Ethel Peterson, Sheila Seaman, Heather Bergeron, Lynn and Dennis Silvernail, John Cramm, Sandy Snyman, Brenda Schisel (dear friend and cousin too), David Sills, Gina Gaetz, Lorraine and Howard Lerner, Cathy Groves, Marnie and Bob Meyers and dear old friend Mara Kier and everyone else whose names might have escaped me. Thank you.

Dr. Martin Luther King Jr. I quote him. "Life's most persistent and urgent question is: What are you doing for others?"

The incredible and special veterinarians, technicians and staff at Northampton Veterinary Clinic in Northampton, MA for their dedication to and more than excellent care of their patients and for so much, much more. You are wonderful and I love you all. I really do!

Andrew Marsh, Dylan Arnould (my grandson) and

Aurora Berman for their much needed technical help while writing this book. I could not have accomplished all that I did without your help. I love you.

Sue Feuerbach, for her more than fantastic editing skills, and helping me to decide which photos to use for this book. Sue entered my life in my very senior years and has made them easier and more joyful.

Rodney Charles and Ed Spinella of 1st World Publishing, two wonderful guys.

Pug Rescue of New England (PRONE) which rescues these adorable little dogs from horrendous abuse and neglect. It was through them that my son and his wife adopted their third pug whom they named Franco, in memory and honor of our beloved Franco. See back cover.

Joey's Greyhound Friends, already mentioned, but not enough. Brigitte rescues Greyhounds from Florida tracks, many of whom are near death. She also rescues abandoned and needy cats. I love you, Brigitte. Greyhound Rescue of Florida, my dear friend Marilyn, who often works with Brigitte. I love you. Greyhound Options in Massachusetts, Claire and Cliff, from whom I've adopted so many former racers. Mr. White is one of them. So much love and thanks to you and your volunteers.

Greyhound Rescue of New England, Diane Henning; Greyhound Action League of Buffalo, Laura Pike; Greyhound Protection League (GPL), Susan Netboy, founder, and PA. representative Kathy Sondej. Thanks also to other Greyhound groups/rescuers whose names I do not know.

Greyhounds In Need (GIN), a registered charity located in Great Britain and founded by Anne and Arthur Finch many, many years ago. It is dedicated to rescuing Greyhounds and especially Galgos. Galgos are Greyhounds bred in Spain and are probably the most persecuted breed of dogs. They are used for hunting hares (an abomination) and their lives are filled with pain and suffering. At the end of each hunting season they are murdered. They are hanged, shot, dumped into abandoned wells and even burned to death. Hard to believe, but true. GIN works with many rescue groups in Spain who do the essential rescue work. Homes then are found for them in Europe. Louise Coleman's Greyhound Friends in Massachusetts has also found homes for Galgos in the United States.

More thanks to:

Life Savers Wild Horse Rescue, Jill Starr; American Wild Horse Sanctuary; American Wild Horse Preservation Campaign; Redwings Horse Rescue and Sanctuary; Healing Hearts Animal Rescue and Refuge, Betty Welton; Bay State Equine Rescue, Equine Advocates, Pryor Wild Horse Range and Fleet of Angels. My friend Elaine Nash, whom I've already discussed in the book, informed me about the latter. It was founded by another Elaine Nash and this group provides transportation to safety throughout the United States and Canada for horses and other equines who are at risk for slaughter. Reccently, two hundred burros were rescued from certain death.

Dr. Pat Haight who, until her untimely death a few years ago, was the Southwest Regional Director of Conquistador Equine Rescue and Advocacy Program, a program of In Defense of Animals (IDA).

In Defense of Animals (IDA) for sponsoring Doll Stanley's Hope Animal Sanctuary in Mississippi. Just recently IDA created another group called Justice for Animals, which Doll Stanley will lead. It was created after a man in Winona, Miss. set his dog on fire and watched as the dog burned to death. His punishment? A three hundred dollar fine. Justice for Animals will work to change the laws in the South that desperately need changing. Two very competent women will lead Hope Animal Sanctuary.

International Primate Protection League (IPPL) Shirley McGreal, Sarasota In Defense of Animals, International

Society for Animal Rights (ISAR), Susan Dapsis, Farm Sanctuary in New York and California, Catskill Animal Sanctuary, Pepper's Place, Rainbow Rescue, Ox N'Yoke Farm Animal Sanctuary, Alley Cat Allies, Animal Dreams, Dakin Humane Society, Berkshire Humane Society, John Perrault; United Poultry Concerns, Karen Davis; Wolf Haven International, Animal People, Friends of Animals (FOA), Priscilla Feral; and Primarily Primates Inc. (PPI), Priscilla Feral.

Friends of Animals and Primarily Primates, Inc. recently adopted three wild horses, two youngsters and a foal, who miraculously survived one of the BLM's many horrendous and lethal wild horse round-ups. They are thriving at Primarily Primates, Inc. A sane society would not include groups such as the Bureau of Land Management.

Little Brook Farm in Old Chatham, N.Y. Friend Elaine Nash made me aware of this group. Established in 1977, it provides sanctuary to horses and other non humans in need.

The Elephant Sanctuary in Tennessee was founded in late 2003. It provides loving and responsible care for elephants who had spent their lives in circuses. All were in desperate need both emotionally and physically. Physical abuse includes the use of bull hooks. For many it takes years of love and medical care before they bond with each other and become life long friends.

The Center for Biological Diversity, whose purpose is to protect our Endangered Earth. I quote: "They All Deserve A Chance. Wild animals great and small – wolves, polar bears, grizzlies, sea turtles and more -are relying on us." Thanks also to Ocean Conservancy and similar organizations.

Native American Heritage Association for providing food, shelter and heat for the original Americans, so many, too many of whom are living in unspeakable poverty. What a disgrace! ROAR (Rescue Operation for Animals on the Reservation). Its name says it all.

SANE! Stop Animal Exploitation Now! – Michael Budkie. SANE! played a huge role in ending animal experiments/vivisection at the Regional Primate Research Center in Southborough, MA. Thank you!

Farm Animal Reform movement founded by Alex Hershaft, a child Holocaust survivor. Mr. Hershaft remembers the cattle cars in which Jews were sent to their slaughter. He says, "I saw a lot of analogies between what the Nazis did to us and what we're doing to farm animals."

The many (but not enough) compassionate and courageous non Jews who risked their and their families' lives by doing the "right thing." They rescued and hid Jews during the Holocaust. They are revered and remembered at Yad Vashem in Israel and by all good persons who are aware of their courage and compassion at a time when compassion and courage were almost non-existent.

The Jewish Foundation for the Righteous, which provides food, shelter and other necessities for these extraordinary persons world-wide. Those who are still alive are quite elderly.

King Mohammed of Morocco who, in 1941, at the age of 32, informed the Vichy French authorities that he disapproved of the anti-Jewish laws. He said he would not follow them. He told them that, as in the past, the Jews would stay under his protection. "........ I refuse any distinction between my subjects." At the end of World War II, Moroccan Jews were safe and secure. If only there were more persons like King Mohammed.

After the Nazis entered Denmark, King Christian wore the Star of David and encouraged his non Jewish citizens to do likewise. Many did. The world needs more persons like him and them.

Nazi hunters after World War II, Beate and Serge Klarsfeld, Simon Wiesenthal and others whose names I do not know.

Elie Wiesel, child holocaust survivor, eloquent writer

and worldwide humanitarian: " I swore never to be silent whenever, wherever, human beings endure suffering and humiliation." He was not.

World Jewish Congress, Ronald Lauder, which fights anti Semitism in the U.S. and world-wide. It should be noted that while good people everywhere fiercely condemn ISIS for its bloody and deadly acts of violence, few condemn the murder and violence inflicted upon Israelis: men, women and children. In fact, messages are placed on Facebook and other similar sites that incite violence by encouraging troubled and vulnerable young persons to murder Israelis. Recently, stabbing has become a popular method. The World Jewish Congress works tirelessly to halt and prevent these atrocities.

The Anti Defamation League (ADL) does the same. Its recently retired president, Abraham Foxman, a Holocaust survivor, has said," The gas chambers in Auschwitz did not begin with bricks; they began with words, with ugly words. Because there was no one who stood up and said, 'Don't say that! I will not be silent.'" He is so right. Positive words lead to positive action; ugly words lead to atrocities. New CEO and National Director is Jonathan Greenblatt.

The Jewish Federation of the Berkshires and similar organizations that provide food and home care to impoverished Jews in the Berkshires, nation-wide and world-wide.

Frank Sinatra, who is known world- wide for his beautiful voice. Few know that he was beautiful inside and outside. His was a life -long commitment to fighting anti -semitism. In the early hours of a day in March 1948, Mr. Sinatra smuggled about one million dollars in cash in a paper bag to an Irish ship captain docked in a port in New York. The money was delivered to Jewish fighters whose passion/goal was to create a Jewish state. It has also been reported that Mr. Sinatra walked out on the christening of his son when the priest refused to allow a Jewish friend to be the infant's god father.

Sar-El, The National Project for Volunteers in Israel. It means Service for Israel, and its volunteers come from countries world-wide and perform essential work. I know because I was a volunteer on a military base many decades ago. It was a most gratifying experience and, with help from a young soldier and the general on the base, a little dog was rescued, spayed and placed in foster care until a permanent home was found. I shall never forget those three weeks.

North American Conference on Ethiopian Jewry, Barbara R. Gordon, New York City, N.Y., provides food, shelter and education in Ethiopia for Ethiopian Jews who are waiting to enter Israel. Although the government of Ethiopia does not persecute its Jewish citizens, the latter live in extreme poverty and their lives are filled with pain and suffering. Many have already emigrated to Israel and many more are waiting to do so. I thank this organization for its wonderful work on behalf of these persons and I thank the state of Israel for welcoming them. Incidentally, several years ago a young Ethiopian Jew was voted Miss Israel. She is quite beautiful.

American Jewish World Service, Ruth Messinger, helps poverty stricken persons in Africa. Its motto: "Pursuing Global Justice. A Jewish Thing to Do."

The Help Sudan Fund founded by the Lost Boys of Sudan "whose goal is to provide food and water to children in Darfur and to build schools to educate the uneducated. Programs include "recruiting school administration, integrating community involvement, providing funding to teachers and administrators, constructing school buildings, and drilling water wells for the school campus."

I learned about this Fund after reading "*Musicians of Darfur*", by Aman Charles, son of 1st World Publishing founder Rodney Charles and Nandini Charles, who sent me copies of Aman's books. Aman was thirteen years old when he wrote this book, which was published in 2015. When he was seven, eight and nine years of age he wrote three books for children, all of them fantastic. Aman, you are very special. You are an exceptionally gifted writer, a compassionate young man and the world needs more persons like you.

One Family Fund helps victims of terrorism in Israel and their families. Magen David Adom provides instant help whenever there are emergencies in Israel and world-wide; ie; terrorism, earthquakes and other natural disasters.

Doctors Without Borders, for saving lives world-wide; Mercy Ships for providing free surgeries and medical care for African children, teens and adults; Smile Train which provides free corrective surgery for children with cleft lips and palates world-wide; Operation Smile and Heal The Children do the same. A dear friend, Jane Bederka, has volunteered with Heal the Children and is fortunate to have experienced the good feelings that come when we help others. Other life-saving organizations are Mercy Corps, which comes to the aid of persons world-wide when disasters strike, ie. earth quakes, deadly conflicts and starvation; Project Hope, which delivers much needed medicines and other supplies and provides health care where needed world-wide; 20/ 20/ 20, which provides free surgeries to erase blindness in persons in poverty stricken countries world-wide, and all other similar life-saving groups whose names I do not know.

The United States Holocaust Memorial Museum, which keeps alive the memory of the Holocaust, fights against other more recent and on-going genocides and helps keep their memories alive. The Museum's wonderful staff and volunteers help the Museum to "confront hatred, prevent genocide and promote human dignity around the world." It educates persons about the Nazi persecution of not just Jews, but of gypsies, homosexuals, the disabled, etc. The Holocaust should have been a warning, but mass atrocities continue world-wide. It reports that Syria has created the largest humanitarian emergency since World War II.

Hospitals in Israel where both Jews and Palestinians receive excellent and compassionate care. The following is taken from an Interview with former Israeli President Shimon Peres, by Peter Geffen in The Jewish Week, January 22, 2016. Asked how he fills his time now that he left politics, Mr. Peres explained: He founded The Peres Center for Peace about twenty years ago. One of its programs is Saving Children. He learned that there were about 2,000 Palestinian children wounded during that period's Intifada. All of them were brought to hospitals in Jerusalem and all of them were cured. After that, parents of Palestinian children who had not been wounded in the war, but who had heart and brain problems, asked for help and received it. The record now is eleven thousand Palestinian children cured in hospitals in Jerusalem. Unfortunately, there are some parents who, when they learn that the hospitals are located in Jerusalem, refuse their help. Their children die. How sad. Prejudice is such a killer.

Other organizations that deserve thanks are Vietnam Veterans Against the War, Iraq Veterans Against the War, Marine Toys for Tots Foundation and other organizations that help veterans and their families. One of the projects of Vietnam Veterans Against the War is to help veterans in Vietnam, their children, grand children, great grand children etc. who are suffering desperately – physically and mentally – from the horrible effects of Agent Orange which was used by American troops without thought to its consequences. American Vietnam veterans and their children and grandchildren are also experiencing the horrible affects of Agent Orange – lack of limbs, cancer and more.

My English teacher who, when I was about fourteen years old, introduced me to a book written by Ashley Montague.

I do not remember its name, but it discussed the fallacy of racism and changed my life forever.

Finally, I thank my parents, Margie (Margaret) and Frank Berk, for their unconditional love and support. My mom was a fantastic soprano, my dad a fantastic pianist who could not read notes. I thought they were the "norm", but later discovered that they were unusual parents and persons. I also thank my paternal grandfather, Isadore Berk, and several aunts and uncles who gifted me with their love, among them Aunt Hilda and Uncle Dave, Uncle Jack, Uncle Mark, Aunt Emily and Aunt Esther. Without all of this unconditional love I would be a lesser person. I also thank my cherished brother Robert, a very talented violinist and violist, who taught me how to play the guitar. To me he was and always will be Bobby. All are deceased.

A Memorable Experience:
When I was ten or eleven years of age I arrived home for lunch one day and when I entered our apartment I was stunned! There in the living room was a beautiful baby grand piano, a gift from my parents. This same beautiful baby grand piano is in my living room as I write.

Fortunately, my children received the same kind of love from my parents, me, Aunt Hilda and Uncle Jack. I know it has infiltrated into their hearts and they have beautiful memories. My adopted son, David entered our lives four months after my father passed away. I had intended to name him Frank, in honor and memory of my dad, but he had already been baptized David in an orphanage in Vietnam. His name is David Frank. He was quite traumatized and desperately needed love, which he received from me, my four other children, my mom and Aunt Hilda. Today he is especially close to my daughter, Vicki. When David entered our lives we had two adorable pugs, Pumkin and Minh. Minh was named by David; in English it means Sunrise.

Finally, I thank non humans everywhere for being in our lives and helping heal us from whatever is hurting us. It would be a better world if more humans treated you with the respect and compassion that is rightfully yours. I am so sorry for the pain and suffering that so many, too many humans inflict upon you. Bless you all.

P.S. Something I have wanted to do for a long, long time but probably never will do: Hug a Pig.

Greta, February 2016

Jonathan and Beth, with their three pugs.

Roman, rescued by dear friend Abby Arnould.

Goldie, Joanne's treasure.
She calls him her lifesaver.

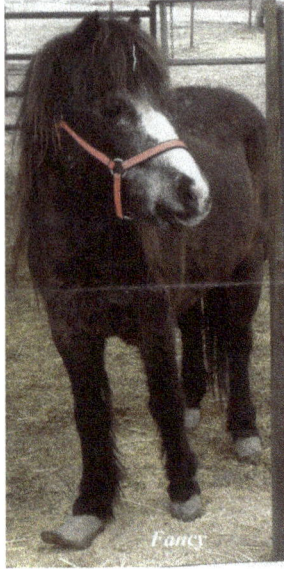

Before

Fancy,
Redwings Horse Rescue and Sanctuary.
Paula Germain, Executive Director.

After

Before

Duke,
Redwings Horse Rescue and Sanctuary.

(After he gained almost 200 pounds)

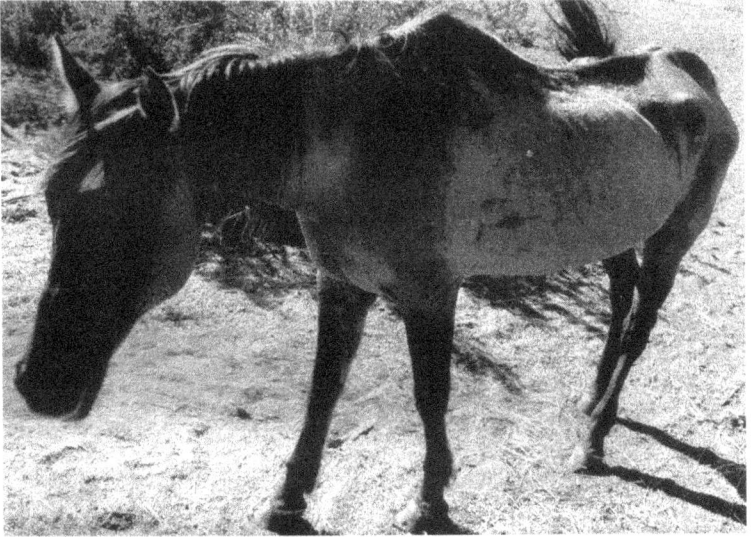

Before

Redwings Horse Rescue and Sanctuary.

After

Farewell to Ginny, Mirage and Gypsy.
Redwings Horse Rescue and Sanctuary.

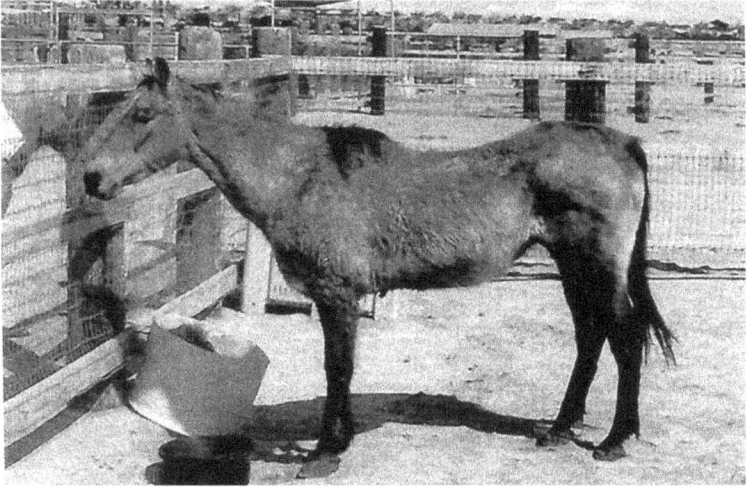

Before

Lifesavers Wild Horse Rescue, Lancaster, CA.
Jill Starr, Founder and Executive Director.

After

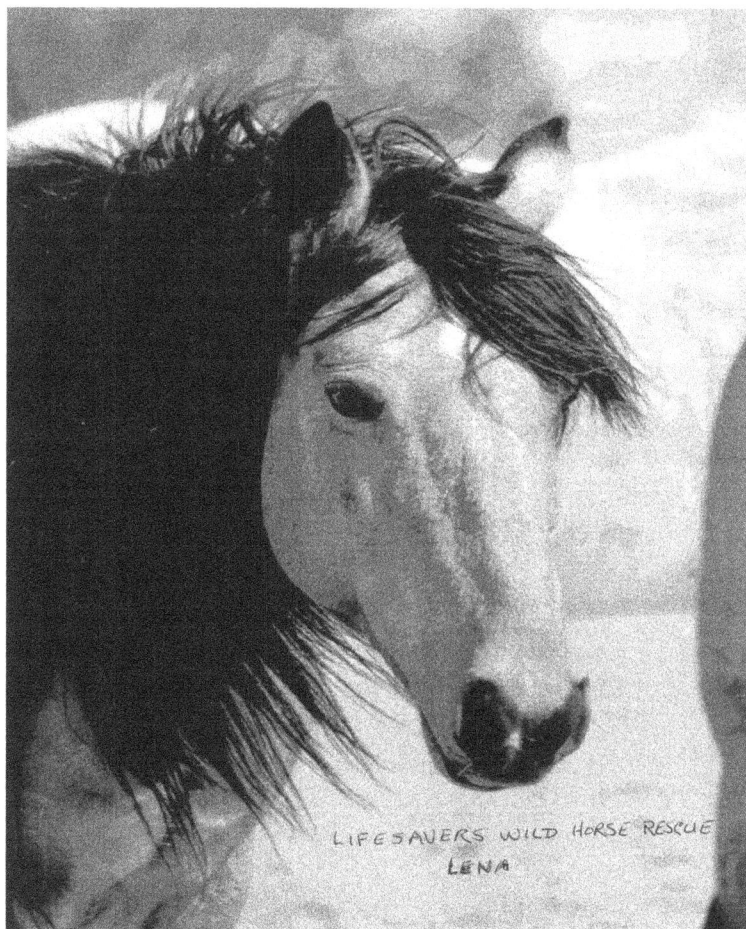

Lena, Lifesavers Wild Horse Rescue, Lancaster, CA.

Lifesavers Wild Horse Rescue
Spring-a-lear was born on the first day of Spring. He is the foal of a
rescued mare who was pregnant. Rescuers did not know that the
mare was pregnant. Two lives were saved.

Lifesavers Wild Horse Rescue

Lifesavers Wild Horse Rescue.

Rescued by Return to Freedom Wild Horse Preservation, Education
and Sanctuary, Lompac, CA.
Photos by Irene Vejar. Neda De Mayo, President.

Rescued by Return to Freedom Wild Horse Preservation,
Education and Sanctuary.
Photos by Irene Vejar.

Rescued by Return to Freedom Wild Horse Preservation,
Education and Sanctuary.
Photos by Irene Vejar.

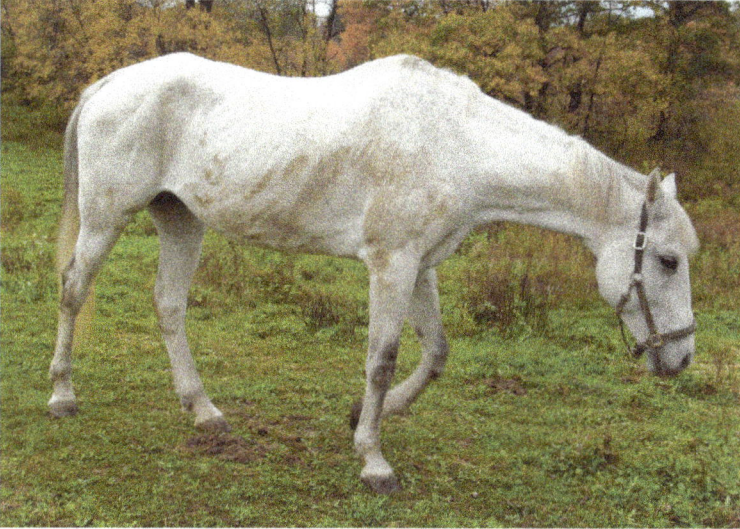

Before rescue: Merlin, a 17-year-old gelding, was rescued by Bay State Equine Rescuer, Susan Sheridan, Principle Officer. He had been sold at an auction house because his human family had been unsatisfied with his endurance trail riding. Large numbers of horses sold at auction die by slaughter.

Merlin after his rescue.

Gina before rescue. Gina was an eleven year old mare when Bay State Equine Rescue was contacted by an animal control officer. She was suffering from many wounds and was about 200 pounds under-weight.

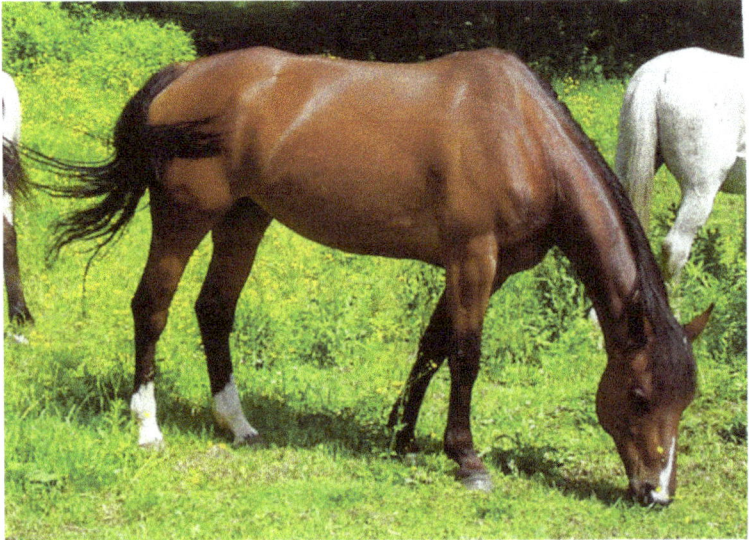

Gina after rescue. Bay State Equine Rescue.

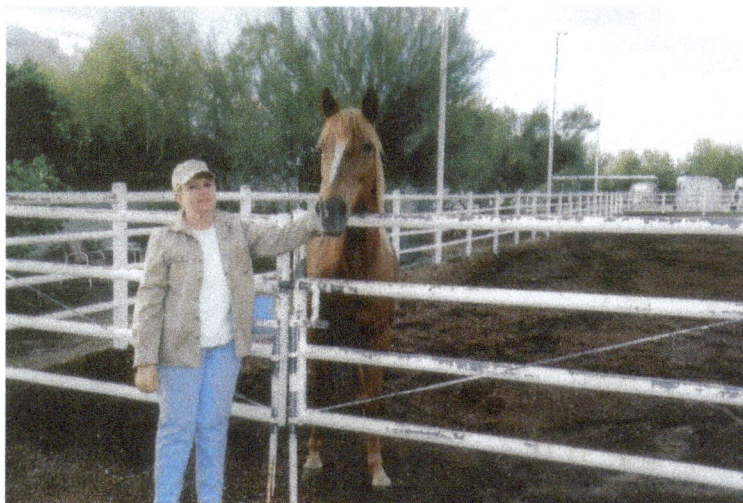

Dr. Pat Haight and Conquistador, one of her rescues. Pat rescued many, many horses. She passed away suddenly and unexpectedly in July 2012. She was only 66 and is missed so very much by her husband Bill and all of us who knew and loved her.

Ione and Greta hold a photo of Ione's deceased husband Franco.

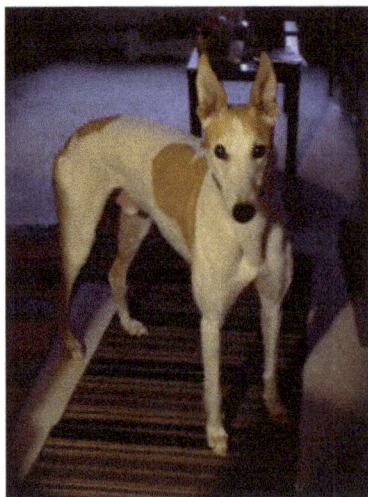

Mr. White, Greta's treasure.

Ione and Mr. White.

Mr. White.

Mr. White and Greta.

About the Author

Since her teenage years, Greta Marsh has been active in the human civil rights movement. Her Master's Thesis was a comprehensive study of racial violence in the United States and the founding of the NAACP (National Association for the Advancement of Colored People) by persons of both races. In August 1963, she participated in Martin Luther King Jr.'s March on Washington for Jobs and Freedom. During that same period, Freedom Riders spent time at her home while they were en route to the deep South.

For many years Greta was a probation officer who worked with troubled, abused and neglected children, battered women and an occasional battered man. She wonders if perhaps men are too embarrassed to report abuse.

In 1980 she crossed the barrier that separates the species and became an advocate not just for human animals, but also for non human animals. She became a vegetarian. Soon after Minh came into her life in November 1994, she became a vegan. Minh's mom was a dairy cow whose male calves are of no use to the dairy industry. Most end up being slaughtered. Some wise and knowledgeable doctors advise that cows' and goats' milk are healthy only for their own babies. Not for humans. Greta's companion dogs have been vegan for a long, long time and were and are healthy and more than just satisfied. Bone cancer, a disease of the dog racing industry, claimed the lives of most of them.

Upon retiring from the Nassau County, N.Y. Probation Department in late 1991, Greta moved to Lanesboro, MA, and started rescuing horses, a calf and some cats. Lovely Shayna is the former racer who inspired and motivated Greta to start the dog racing ban in MA. It was a 17 year battle that changed her life forever.

Greta is the mother of five children, the grand-mother of ten and a recent great grandmother. Margaret, one of her beautiful granddaughters, gave birth to a little girl on December 7, 2015. She and Adam, her husband, named the baby Greta. Quite a compliment! Greta the elder and her cherished companion, Mr. White, live in Easthampton, MA.

More Books by Greta Marsh

The Story of My Life – by Shayna as Told to Greta

Frankie and Jonny and Mommy Too

www.ingramcontent.com/pod-product-compliance
Lightning Source LLC
Chambersburg PA
CBHW050818090426
42737CB00021B/3423